The Die
Is Cast

The Die
Is Cast

Arkansas Goes to War, 1861

Edited by
Mark K. Christ

Contributors:
Michael B. Dougan
Lisa Tendrich Frank
Carl Moneyhon
Thomas A. DeBlack
William Garrett Piston

BUTLER
CENTER

BOOKS

Little Rock, Arkansas

**BUTLER
CENTER**

The Butler Center for Arkansas Studies
Central Arkansas Library System
100 Rock Street
Little Rock, Arkansas 72201

BOOKS

First Edition, March 2010

ISBN 978-1-935106-15-9 (10-digit ISBN 1-935106-15-5)

10 9 8 7 6 5 4 3 2 1

Project manager: Rod Lorenzen
Book design and cover design: H. K. Stewart
Copyeditor: Ali Welky

The editor secured the photographs and illustrations used in this book.

Library of Congress Cataloging-in-Publication Data

The die is cast : Arkansas goes to war, 1861 / edited by Mark K. Christ ; contributors, Michael B. Dougan ... [et al.]. -- 1st ed.
     p. cm.
  Includes bibliographical references and index.
  ISBN-13: 978-1-935106-15-9 (pbk. : alk. paper)
  ISBN-10: 1-935106-15-5 (pbk. : alk. paper)
  1. Arkansas--History--Civil War, 1861-1865. 2. Secession--Arkansas. 3. Arkansas--Politics and government--1861-1865. I. Christ, Mark K. II. Dougan, Michael B., 1944- III. Title.

E471.57.D54 2010
973.709767--dc22

2009043858

Printed in the United States of America

This book is printed on archival-quality paper that meets requirements of the American National Standard for Information Sciences, Permanence of Paper, Printed Library Materials, ANSI Z39.48-1984.

Table of Contents

Contributors

Michael B. Dougan taught at Arkansas State University from 1970 until his recent retirement. He is the author of many articles and books, including *Confederate Arkansas: The People and Policies of a Frontier State in Wartime* (1976); *Arkansas Odyssey: The Saga of Arkansas from Prehistoric Times to Present* (1994); and *Community Diaries: Arkansas Newspapering, 1819–2002* (2003). A past president of the Arkansas Historical Association and recipient of the Lifetime Achievement Award, he endeavors to go canoeing on New Year's Day.

Lisa Tendrich Frank received her PhD from the University of Florida in 2001. She has published several articles on the experiences of women during the Civil War, and she is currently working on *Women and the Civil War: An Encyclopedia* and *Home Fires Burning: The Gendered Implications of Sherman's March*. She has taught at several universities around the country, including the University of California, Los Angeles; Occidental College; the University of North Florida; and Florida Atlantic University.

Carl Moneyhon is a professor of history at the University of Arkansas at Little Rock, specializing in Southern U.S. history and the Civil War and Reconstruction. He received his BA and MA from the University of Texas and his PhD from the University of Chicago. A prolific writer and researcher, he published *Texas after the Civil War: The Struggle of Reconstruction* (2004), *Arkansas and the New South, 1874–1929* (1997), and *The Impact of the Civil War and Reconstruction on Arkansas* (1994). Moneyhon also served as a general editor of the University of Arkansas Press's award-winning series *Portraits of Conflict*, having also co-authored three of these impressive photo journals.

7

Thomas A. DeBlack is an associate professor of history at Arkansas Tech University in Russellville. He holds a BA from Southern Methodist University, an MSE from Ouachita Baptist University, and a PhD from the University of Arkansas. DeBlack taught in the public schools in Arkansas for twelve years. He is a past president of the Arkansas Historical Association and the Arkansas Association of College History Teachers. He is co-author of *Arkansas: A Narrative History* (University of Arkansas Press, 2002), and author of *With Fire and Sword: Arkansas 1861–1874* (University of Arkansas Press, 2003). In 2003, *Arkansas: A Narrative History* was named the winner of the Arkansas Library Association's Arkansiana Prize, and *With Fire and Sword* was the first winner of the Butler-Remmel Arkansas History Literary Prize.

William Garrett Piston teaches at Missouri State University in Springfield, Missouri, where he specializes in American military history and the Civil War and Reconstruction. He received his BA and MA degrees from Vanderbilt University and his PhD from the University of South Carolina. Piston's scholarship has won awards from the Center for Studies in Military History, the State Historical Society of Missouri, the Sons of Confederate Veterans, the United Daughters of the Confederacy, the Colonial Dames of America, and Missouri State University. The author or co-author of two books, twenty-one articles, and two booklets, he is best known for his 1987 work *Lee's Tarnished Lieutenant: James Longstreet and His Place in Southern History*, a revisionist history of a controversial Confederate general. Piston's most recent work is *Wilson's Creek: The Second Battle of the Civil War and the Men Who Fought It* (co-authored with Richard Hatcher), published in March 2000. The State Historical Society of Missouri recognized Piston with its Missouri History Book Award in 2001 for *Wilson's Creek*.

Mark K. Christ is community outreach director for the Arkansas Historic Preservation Program and organizer of the Old State House Museum's Civil War seminars. A 1982 graduate of the University of Arkansas at Little Rock, he received his master's degree in 2000 from the University of Oklahoma. He has edited several books, including *Rugged and Sublime: The Civil War in Arkansas*; *Sentinels of History: Reflections on Arkansas Properties Listed on the National Register of Historic Places*, which won an Award of Merit from the American Association for State and Local History; *Getting Used to Being Shot At: The Spence Family Civil War Letters*; *"All Cut to Pieces and Gone to Hell": The Civil War, Race Relations, and the Battle of Poison Spring*; and *The Earth Shook and Trees Trembled: Civil War Arkansas 1863–1864*. The University of Oklahoma Press will publish his next book, *Civil War Arkansas, 1863: The Battle for a State*, in 2010.

Introduction

On August 19, 2006, the Old State House Museum in Little Rock hosted a seminar, "The Die is Cast: Arkansas Goes to War, 1861," that brought experts from around the country to explore why a small frontier state, a part of the Union for only twenty-five years, would choose to sever its ties with the United States and join the southern Confederacy.

The speakers examined the political and social forces that led to secession, transforming farmers, clerks, and shopkeepers into soldiers. Long-time Arkansas State University professor Michael Dougan delved into the 1861 Arkansas Secession Convention and the delegates' internal divisions on whether to leave the Union. Lisa Tendrich Frank of Florida Atlantic University discussed the role Southern women played in moving the state toward secession, while Carl Moneyhon of the University of Arkansas at Little Rock looked at the factors that led peaceful civilians to join the army. Thomas A. DeBlack of Arkansas Tech University told of the thousands of Arkansawyers who chose not to follow the Confederate banner in 1861, and William Garrett Piston of Missouri State University chronicled the first combat experience of the green Arkansas troops at Wilson's Creek. Collectively, these essays provide an overview of the diverse passions that brought the people of Arkansas to war.

Many people contributed to the symposium and publication of this book. Bill Gatewood, Georganne Sisco, Gail Moore, Rita Wilson, Joellen Maack, Amy Peck, and Ian Beard of the Old State House Museum were all deeply involved in the seminar, and the museum helped to underwrite this publication. David Stricklin, Brian Robertson, Rod Lorenzen, and Ali Welky of the Butler Center for Arkansas Studies, Central Arkansas Library System, in

Little Rock, provided guidance and assistance in publishing the proceedings of the seminar. S. Charles Bolton made suggestions that improved the manuscript considerably. Many others provided assistance throughout both projects, and, though they are not named here, their aid is no less appreciated.

Mark K. Christ
March 18, 2008

"An eternal chitter chatter kept up in the galleries": The Arkansas Secession Convention in Action, March–June, 1861

Michael B. Dougan

On March 4, 1861, the newly elected president, Abraham Lincoln, delivered his first inaugural address. In it he told the nation that the "momentous issue of civil war" rested with the people, not with him. In Little Rock, a newly assembled convention received these words by telegraph and did not find them reassuring. Historians tend to focus on the impact these words had on the political classes, but the history of Arkansas during this time plainly reveals that many failed to grasp what was about to take place. Whether it was "chitter chatter" in the convention's gallery or later the *"shoals"* of young women on horseback who ignored Little Rock's overflowing collection of sick and wounded soldiers, many missed the momentous nature of the unfolding events. Disengagement from the crises of the day is not new to Arkansas.

In the summer and fall of 1860, Arkansas voters had been thoroughly misled by the state's Democratic leadership. First, the party pretended that John C. Breckinridge, the Southern Democrat, was a national nominee; second, it minimized the potential election of Abraham Lincoln by asserting that alarmist rhetoric was merely another in the ongoing series of political crises that had distressed the nation since the acquisition of lands from Mexico reenergized the slavery question. While supporters of national Democrat

Stephen A. Douglas and ex-Whigs operating out of a shell organization called the Constitutional Union Party under John Bell tried to educate the voters on the gravity of the situation, the backward and parochial nature of half the state's counties had proven, as it generally always has been, too great an obstacle to overcome.[1]

On November 6, a day that Camden diarist John W. Brown called "the most important day to these United States and perhaps to mankind since the Fourth of July 1776," Breckinridge carried Arkansas over Bell and Douglas, although the turnout was 7,000 below what it had been in the election for governor in August, and only some 3,000 votes separated Breckinridge from the combined Bell/Douglas count. Rather than being a referendum on the desirability of a civil war, the vote recapitulated the Whig/ Democratic alignments of the past twenty years. Breckinridge's areas of strongest support would become the best recruiting grounds for the Federal army. With voting done by voice instead of paper ballots, Republican Abraham Lincoln received only a handful of votes.[2] Of course Lincoln's election had been South Carolina's goal, and that state passed an ordinance of secession on December 20, 1860, even though Lincoln would not become president until March 4, 1861.[3]

Reactions to the hardly stunning election results ran a gamut. The upland peoples, whose counties—their "Little Kingdoms"—formed almost the sum total of their world, knew little and cared less, and were more interested that come first frost, it was hog-butchering time. By contrast, the planters, who as a class had supported Bell or Douglas, saw that forces out of their hands were likely to impel them into times of economic uncertainty. The state's political establishment, the "Family" or "Dynasty," now led by retiring U.S. senator Robert Ward Johnson, had suffered a major defeat that summer when maverick Democrat Henry Massie Rector had bested Richard Mentor Johnson in the gubernatorial campaign. Senator Johnson, who had opposed the Compromise of 1850, now called on Arkansans to follow South Carolina and assembled a coalition that consisted of his former bitter enemy, Congressman Thomas Carmichael Hindman, as well as Albert Pike, the former Whig and Know-Nothing leader, and a parcel of lesser figures.[4] Curious indeed was the reaction of outgoing governor Elias Nelson Conway, who thought the whole crisis to be the result of British bribery and corruption.[5] Equally remote from reality were the ideas of incoming governor Henry Massie Rector.

While still a minor, Rector came to Arkansas, leaving behind his mother and stepfather and hoping to further his father's land claim to a part of what would become Hot Springs. There were a number of other Rector cousins in Arkansas, who in turn were connected by marriage with the Conways, Johnsons, and Seviers. Through his kinship connection, Rector certainly qualified as a Family member eligible for patronage positions, but only dead-end jobs came his way. Short-lived was his position as teller at the soon-to-become-defunct State Bank, and no one with any desire to have clean hands would have accepted an appointment as federal marshal from the Tyler administration.[6] Rector seems to have spent much of the late 1840s and early 1850s trying to avoid paying his debts, but as his financial position stabilized, he began to make some threatening political noises. A brief stint on the state Supreme Court revealed his ignorance of the law but did not placate his now bounding ambition. Seeing a chance in the turmoil created by Richard Mentor Johnson's gubernatorial nomination in the spring of 1860, and with no other organized opposition, Rector had plunged in, announcing himself as an Independent Democrat.[7]

Although no paper trail exists, apparently Thomas Hindman encouraged the move. Overextended financially, Hindman had thought that he had married an heiress, but that proved to be a mistake. Then a series of political mishaps had damaged him during the previous year. One of his chief expenses was the *Old Line*

Democrat. Rector probably paid Hindman for its use during the gubernatorial campaign, and its editor, Thomas C. Peek, thereafter married one of Rector's nieces. The obvious move would have been for Hindman to unload the newspaper on Rector. But this seemingly easy transfer of ownership did not take place, perhaps because Rector was outbid by the much wealthier Johnsons. Another problem was that Rector could not or would not work with anybody. "Henry is a violent man and fights people," William Minor "Cush" Quesenbury had observed shortly after Rector made his announcement. Quesenbury, who had known Rector for years, was correct in his assessment. Peek stayed with Rector, but following Hindman's peace with the Family, the *Old Line Democrat* shut down by the end of 1860. Rector knew he was naked without a newspaper before a hostile political world. Rector's private secretary, Dr. J. J. Gaines, created for the governor a short-lived organ called the *Southern States.* However, for most of 1861, Rector had no newspaper to defend him. Finally, in the fall of 1861, the redoubtable Peek, whom the governor had given a state job, began publishing the *Daily State Journal.*[8] Rector's inauguration was clearly the highwater mark of his career, when, as a Little Rock diarist put it, "the long procession of little 'niggers' and noisy boys marched up to the governor's splendid mansion and 'liquored.'"[9]

Rector's first step into political oblivion came on November 15, 1860, when his address to the legislature moved from a long list of routine items to his venting one of his specious but obdurately held arguments, namely that it was unconstitutional for the North to have "revolutionized the government." Rector attempted to lead the nascent secessionist movement, but the legislature ignored, for example, his arguments against filling the vacancy in the U.S. Senate. Rector's proclamation on December 12, 1860, offered another example of the governor's advanced thinking. In it he urged that slave owners from other states should be prohibited from moving slaves into Arkansas unless they intended to settle. This measure, he confidently asserted, would "compel the border states to take care and protect their own slave property."[10]

The actual secession convention bill came from Ben T. Du Val of Fort Smith. A long-time resident of Arkansas (and childhood schoolmate of William Minor Quesenbury), Du Val was virtually the only Democrat of note associated with Governor Rector. The pronounced disinclination of the legislature to act led the secessionists to urge that the issue be turned over to the people in a referendum. Rhetorical cries of this sort played out in the state press until December 21, when Senator Johnson and Congressman Hindman endorsed the convention idea from Washington. Albert Pike and James Yell carried the banner back in Arkansas, and a petition drive, mostly from the southern counties, was begun. "The Demon of secession is daily becoming more powerful," Camden diarist John W. Brown observed. The lower house passed the bill on December 22, but the state Senate did not act until January 16, 1861, and only after its numbers had become depleted as members from northern counties headed home thinking the session was virtually over. Instead, the bill was called up and passed. The law authorized voters to decide either for or against calling a convention while at the same time electing delegates should one be approved. This stacked the deck against the anti-secessionists, and Judge David Walker of Fayetteville, a powerful force in the "Great Northwest," for one, called the wording an outrage.[11]

However, the voters did not tread calmly to the polls on February 18, 1861 (the same day that saw Jefferson Davis inaugurated as the provisional president of the Confederate States of America). Instead, the weeks prior to the voting were punctuated by a crisis in Little Rock that had the potential to reach well beyond the bounds of the state. Just exactly what happened to trigger the arsenal crisis was controversial at the time and has remained so.

Suffice it to say that the arrival of telegraph lines linking Little Rock to Memphis on January 28 was followed by John M. Harrell's message reporting a rumor that reinforcements were headed for the arsenal then containing Little Rock native Captain James Totten's caretaker force of 60 men. Subsequent rumors put the supposed reinforcements at 300 or 400 men, and even placed them on the steamboat *S.H. Tucker*. Rector informed Totten that receiving any reinforcements would be an act of war and that this federal army officer would not be permitted to carry off federal army weapons. But adding to the crisis, messages were sent out, presumably under the governor's authority, asking for volunteers to help secure the capital and seize the arsenal. Interestingly, the volunteers, more than a thousand, came mainly from nine plantation counties. The arriving volunteers found Little Rock peaceful, while their governor, now faced with the likelihood that his spontaneous civilian aggrandizement might rise from the level of rhetorical posturing to possible bullets, disavowed making any call and even called out the Pulaski County militia to help keep order.

Totten, of course, was not in a position to resist a physical attack—the arsenal was a storage facility, not a fort in a harbor. And Little Rock itself was strongly pro-Union. The crisis ended with Totten's evacuation, "to avoid the cause of civil war" as this future Union general phrased it, and with Rector becoming the receiver for the cache of arms stored there. Ralph Goodrich best described the event as a drunken frolic financed by the state and led by Governor Rector.[12]

The political ramifications were important. In the plantation counties, persons planning to vote (*viva voce*) against the convention were threatened with physical violence. Elsewhere, revulsion against the seizure strengthened the anti-secessionists. Moreover, it led to the emergence of an anti-secession network that soon took on most of the characteristics of a party. Northwest Arkansas was over-represented in talent, for David Walker of Fayetteville and Jesse Turner of Van Buren were two of the great pioneers of the region, but younger men, whose careers and fame lay in the future, were active as well. William Meade Fishback of Fort Smith and Augustus Hill Garland of Little Rock both would become governors. Christopher Columbus Danley, the proprietor of the *Arkansas State Gazette*, was another key player. His absence—in New York buying arms for the state along with Thomas J. Churchill—had precluded any continuation of the strong editorial writing he had displayed before January, but the centrality of the venerable *Gazette* in the state's political culture gave the movement more than just an organ; for most of its long life, this newspaper transcended ink and paper—it was a spiritual force. The strength of Danley's writing during this period would not be equaled until the world's focus turned to Little Rock in the middle of the next century. By contrast, the leading Democratic and now secessionist newspaper, the *True Democrat*, had long ago displayed its colors and for the most part had become predictably fire-eating.[13]

A total of 43,238 voters—less by 10,000 the vote in November and far fewer than the 59,469 of the August election—endorsed calling a convention by a two-to-one margin. But they elected to it a majority of what can best be styled as "conditional" Unionists. This body chose David Walker as its president, and by a five-vote majority, these Unionists controlled the body, preventing any act of immediate secession. One of the most striking features of the convention was the virtual anonymity of its members. Nowhere to be found were former governors, congressmen, or senators. Josiah Gould, for example, is remembered by legal historians because he authored *Gould's Digest*; Charles W. Adams may have been to his contemporaries a "Pike the second," but his main claim to minor fame is being one of the generals to whom Helena lays claim. James Yell, the onetime Know-Nothing gubernatorial candidate, was the nephew of Archibald Yell, the state's first charismatic, but this trait did not pass over to that side of the family. Of course, one reason for the shortage was that Arkansas had but few elder statesmen living, but the absence of veteran political players still warrants attention. What experience there was could be found on the Unionist side, and that in part explains much of the subsequent chain of events. Yell, who headed up the secession caucus only with difficulty, had to rule in that body that the arsenal issue was out of order, so divisive had this matter become.[14]

This first session of the convention was marked by much windy oratory. During the first days, delegate A. H. Carrigan recalled, "the pressure was intense … and all kinds of raillery came from the lobbies. The galleries and lobbies were always crowded and it was constantly feared that violence might occur, and at times it looked as if it were inevitable." One of the speakers was the governor himself. While the Southern hagiographic position is that slavery had nothing to do with the war, Rector flat-out asserted: "They believe slavery is sin, and we do not, and there lies the trouble."[15] But boredom soon set in. James Yell, "a very strong man without much cultivation," gave what the *True Democrat* (surely tongue in cheek) described as a "mild, classic and elevated discourse," only to be overwhelmed by "an eternal chitter chatter kept up in the galleries."[16]

The convention was important enough that the Confederacy sent a commissioner—Williamson S. Oldham, a former Arkansan who had skipped off to Texas after the banking collapse. Oldham, who arrived near the first session's end, threatened Arkansas with an economic boycott by the new Confederacy if the state did not immediately secede. Oldham changed no votes, and whether anyone took his threat seriously cannot be ascertained, but, New Orleans was less important to Arkansas commercially than St. Louis, Louisville, and Cincinnati. An Arkansas outside the CSA but connected by rail to these entrepôts would have freed the state from the baleful influence of that cancerous center of sin to the infinite improvement of the state's morals and future economic prospects. The voting that followed Oldham's speech produced more speeches, bouquets from the galleries, and cheers for both sides, but, by a vote of 39 to 35, secession was rejected.[17]

What followed was significant. The convention did not adjourn on March 18 but continued sitting—with anti-secessionists allowing themselves to be blackmailed. Threatened by the secession of the southern Arkansas counties, they agreed to refer the issue directly to the people in an August election. Secessionists were pushing for the division of the state, a move that, had it been granted, would have created a much stronger and more coherent Arkansas, and doubtless would be considered a blessing today. However, as Danley and others pointed out, dividing the state was full of constitutional and legal obstacles. County sovereignty, although strong in practice and later enacted into state law, had no legal foundation in American or English history.[18]

Over the next two days, a compromise emerged. Centermost was an agreement that secession would be referred to the voters in August. The convention agreed to elect delegates to work with the border states and adopted a series of resolutions calling for compromise and peace. However, in what was a major victory for the secessionists, the convention pledged to oppose any coercion. Curiously, the coercion the convention secessionists had in mind had to come only from the national government. The South, which had written God into its constitution, could not possibly be an aggressor nation.

After the convention adjourned—with the proviso that its president could call the body back into session—a half-hearted political campaign got under way as if the August election held some meaning. Sectional and economic issues within the state got considerable play. Delegate I. H. Hilliard from Chicot County revived the idea of intra-state secession, observing that, "Unfortunately, our state is divided into two sections whose pursuits are totally dissimilar—the grain and stock-raising portion looks with no friendly eye on the cotton planter." A further characterization came from the *Chicot Press*, which called the people of the upland areas bigoted and ignorant. By contrast, a broadside that circulated in northwest Arkansas asked whether non-slaveholders would be allowed to vote in the new Confederacy. All this extensive rhetoric helped lay the foundation for the "rich slave owner's war, poor man's fight" argument that emerged a year later.[19] Jesse Turner, upon arriving back in Van Buren, was serenaded by that town's famous band. A musical war broke out in Little Rock, with both Unionists and secessionists writing dueling lyrics set to the tunes of "Dixie" and "Look for the Wagon." Meanwhile, of course, events were playing out in Charleston Harbor that determined the course of the next four years.

News of the firing on Fort Sumter did not come in the form of a materially correct and unbiased chronology of the events. Any examination of the newspaper headlines of the period and readings of the first telegraphic dispatches makes it clear that "spin" was being placed on the events that ignored the fact that South Carolina fired the first shot. Modern historians understand what happened, although they may differ in how they interpret the results. But people at the time took what the telegraphic dispatches and newspaper headlines said at face value, at least initially. In fact, the Southern understanding of the firing episode marks the beginning of the creation of what in time emerged as the official Southern cultural legend. A recent scholarly study that takes seriously the rife rumor world of the Confederacy quotes this observation: "a legend is a rumor that has become part of the verbal heritage of a people."[20] In time, while Confederate sympathizers had to admit that the South had shot first, they still claimed it was all the North's fault. It took some time for an alternate (and more accurate) version to surface, but the Peace Society movement in Arkansas and other border states rested on this foundation. "The South commenced it and the South may fight it out," a saying heard all over northern and western Arkansas, shows how limited was the ideology of Southern nationalism.[21]

One very evident problem often glossed over is that only states'-rights Democrats believed in the theoretical existence of the doctrine called secession—the right of a state constitutionally, legally, and peaceably to leave the Union. Ironic it was that Whigs used the occasion to reprint Democratic president Andrew Jackson's stern strictures to South Carolina thirty years earlier. Whigs still tended to argue instead that leaving the Union was justified by a right of revolution. David Walker, the state's leading Whig, must have been galled when he had to call back the convention to pass an act of secession.

And while Walker acted only reluctantly and under considerable pressure, many of his constituents repudiated his action. He and other hard-shell Unionists wanted the border states to act in concert, and it is germane to this to see elements of a position taken more forcibly in Kentucky and Missouri, namely that neutrality was the best course.

Meanwhile, even as Walker pondered, Rector sprang into action, ordering Colonel Solon Borland, recently returned to the state from a spree of newspaper editing in Memphis, to head up four companies of volunteers to seize Fort Smith, an action spurred by another of those great rumors of reinforcements arriving. The volunteers were much "gratified" (said one private) to find the enemy gone, and the riotous trip resulted in a claim against the state for $500 in damages to the steamboat.[22]

For Union men, even if they had converted from conditional Unionism to reluctant secessionism, Rector had driven another nail into his coffin. By contrast, secessionist leader Robert Ward

Johnson had been all for reconciliation since the convention first adjourned. Others might pound away with fire, but Johnson, who had foreseen these events as inevitable back in 1850 when he opposed the compromise of that year, had begun building ties to the other side. Thus when Editor Danley wrote Unionist delegate W. W. Mansfield, "I think the conservative men of the convention should take charge of the affairs of the state and prevent the wild secessionists from sending us the Devil," he was referring to Rector, not Johnson.[23]

Since Arkansas was still receiving dispatches from Washington, President Abraham Lincoln's secretary of war, Simon Cameron, asked the governor for 780 men "to suppress combinations." This gave Rector his one moment of untarnished glory, for repeated in numerous history books was his reply: "In answer to your requisition for troops Arkansas to subjugate the Southern States, I have to say that none will be furnished. The demand is only adding insult to injury. The people of this commonwealth are freemen, not slaves, and will defend to the last extremity their honor, lives, and property against Northern mendacity and usurpation."[24] Heroic words but factually incorrect: more than 5,000 Arkansans served in the Union army, and less than a third of the Arkansas soldiers on the Confederate side were with their units to the last extremity; slaves, who accounted for one quarter of the state's population, were already held in bondage; and Arkansas was not in law a commonwealth. Still, this has remained Rector's claim to fame.

At the time, however, Rector had other worries. "Col. Webb says that when the convention meets they will try to declare my office vacant. Oh Hell," he scribbled on a note. And indeed, deposing the governor was on the minds of many of the delegates.[25]

The first business, however, was passing an ordinance of secession. Perhaps the most exciting moment in the Old State House's history (with the murder in 1837 on the House floor of

Unionist David Walker from northwest Arkansas served as chairman of the acrimonious secession convention that voted to remove Arkansas from the Union. Courtesy of the Shiloh Museum of Ozark History/P-2275.

Representative Anthony being principal competition) started on May 6 at ten o'clock in the morning[26] when David Walker called the convention to order. There was no "chitter chatter" in the galleries or on the floor or even among the boys perched on the windowsills. But then the convention adjourned until that afternoon, and the whole thing had to be done again. W. P. Grace from Pine Bluff, who during Reconstruction asserted that he was really a Negro, made the motion that the state secede. There were no speeches. A. W. Dinsmore from the northwest offered an amendment to refer the matter to voters. By a 55 to 15 vote, the amendment was tabled. Then came the vote, with only five of the delegates daring amongst the overwhelmingly pro-secessionist crowd to vote "nay." Chairman Walker then pled for unanimity, but Isaac Murphy, the horse-collar astronomer from Madison County, refused to change his vote. The boos and hisses were intense, but, in the midst of the frightening noise, Mrs. Frederick Trapnall from on high sent a last bouquet of flowers flying down to the embattled future governor.

The former Unionists had either been converted or overwhelmed but only on the single issue of passing a secession ordinance.[27] What remained was what to do with Governor Rector. During the first session, the convention had gotten involved in the question of who was the Fulton County representative. Since the first election had ended in a tie, the convention ordered the governor to issue instructions for a new election. This he had refused to do, undertaking instead the very risky business of telling the convention, which held in its collective hands the sovereignty of the people of the state of Arkansas, what he thought they could and could not do. So, with secession out of the way, would the convention now depose the governor? And if so, how? Many backroom discussions followed, for a number of the secessionists were of one mind with the former Unionists on the Rector problem.

The first issue concerned military matters. As governor, Rector controlled the militia, and two of the leading secessionists, James Yell and Napoleon Bonaparte Burrow, had been elevated to command positions. Burrow, then at Fort Smith, irked Danley at the *Gazette*, who found this militia officer "so extravagant and so pompously unmilitary as to render the pronunciamentoes and home wars of Mexico almost respectable." Hence, the convention set about creating the Arkansas Army for home defense. Next they destroyed the governor's monopoly on the military power by entrusting it to the three-man Military Board. Its members included the governor but also Family supporter B. C. Totten and the disabled Mexican War veteran Danley. Believing they had solved the main problem, they moved further only by indirection.[28]

Who was responsible for this stop-gap measure? Later, Richard Mentor Johnson claimed that he and other Family members had saved Rector. Hindman reportedly wrote the actual convention draft, although James Yell also claimed credit, observing that it was done "to divert their minds" from more extreme measures.

Rector was not happy, and when the commander selected for the western section, West Point graduate N. Bart Pearce, turned in his militia resignation, Rector refused to accept it, asking Pearce to "define your authority." Pearce replied, logically, that the convention was his authority, and Rector in turn told the convention that he, not it, was commander-in-chief. After having set himself upon a collision course with that body, Rector concluded his letter by promising to "cooperate cheerfully and zealously with the convention in all things!"[29]

Equally botched was the governor's next move. It was two weeks after the passage of the ordinance of session, but the convention showed no signs of going home. The "chitter chatter" in the galleries doubtless had given way to utter silence. Hence, Rector probably sought to speed their departure by summoning the legislature. There was a certain logic to this, for much of what was occupying the delegates' time was more befitting the House and Senate than a convention, but whatever desire a majority of the delegates had to go home stopped when faced with this threat from the governor. Johnson at the *True Democrat* warned that if Rector proceeded, it could be "the most unfortunate step of his life." The convention followed with a formal request for the governor to forbear, and again Rector backed down.[30]

Meanwhile, work went ahead on drafting a new constitution. The new organic document failed to include any reference to God, provided what amounted to a bill of rights for both white men and Native Americans, and scheduled new elections, notably the governor's office, for the following year. Gone was the ban on banking (Amendment 1 to the constitution of 1836). It was, in short, one giant step forward for modernization but taken at the wrong time. Further proof of the persistent Whiggery of the new constitution came when state elections were moved from August to October. Democrats always favored August so that all their shoeless voters could turn out. Whigs, who usually wore shoes, favored October because many Democratic voters would be too busy harvesting crops to bother to vote.[31]

Meanwhile, members were slowly departing. Isaac Murphy did not stay around long enough to sign the new document on June 1, but Archibald Ray, the hunter from Pike County, Samuel "Parson" Kelly of the Kellyites, and two future governors, Harris Flanagin and William M. Fishback, signed off on it. Augustus H. Garland, elected to the Confederate congress, had resigned his seat, but George C. Watkins promptly won a special election to fill it. Finally, after a motion to adjourn failed, enough delegates, led by chairman David Walker, and including delegates from both sides of the aisle, as it were, offered their resignations. With Watkins filling the chair in the absence of Walker and without a quorum, the convention came to an end.

The actions undertaken by the convention greatly influenced the course of the war in Arkansas. While vote for secession was inevitable under the circumstances, the plan for minimizing the governor failed. Rector managed to convert B. C. Totten, one of the Military Board members, to his states'-rights point of view, with the result that the Arkansas Army was never fully transferred into Confederate service. Funding for this soon-disbanded military force crippled state finances, and soldiers, especially those who saw service at the Battle of Wilson's Creek (Oak Hills), were not likely to re-enlist. The resultant disorganization in Arkansas certainly worked against General Earl Van Dorn when that less-than-worthy officer came to Arkansas. The long-running wars first between Rector and the convention and then between Rector and the Confederate authorities over troop transfers may have added fuel to the Peace Society movement during the fall of 1861, and they certainly created a disorganized climate for newly arriving Confederate commander Earl Van Dorn, thus contributing to the Confederate defeat at Pea Ridge (a.k.a. Elkhorn Tavern).[32]

The long hand of the convention remained alive a year later. The subtle clause that relieved Rector of two years of his office was upheld by the state Supreme Court. All of Rector's enemies united around former Whig Harris Flanagin, then serving as a colonel in Tennessee, and soon saw him voted into the governor's office. Flanagin had many fine qualities, but dynamic leadership was not among them. He was in office less than a year when, after the fall of Vicksburg, a Union army made its way up the Arkansas River and Little Rock fell under Yankee control for the rest of the war. Arkansas had become a largely failed state. Flanagin proved not to be the man of the hour, but his sterling integrity made him a player during Reconstruction, and he signed an early draft of the constitution of 1874 before his death soon after. The first governor elected under the Redeemer banner was Augustus H. Garland, the former convention member. Garland epitomized the process by which pasteurized, persistent Whigs, called even in 1861 "conservatives," remade the Democratic Party while keeping the name Democrat. These New Departure Democrats held sway until overwhelmed by first the agrarian revolt and then the rise of that quintessential demagogue, Jeff Davis.

The "chitter chatter" might have ended, but the detachment from the events playing out daily did not. Doctor Junius Bragg later reported that the young ladies of Little Rock soon abandoned caring for the sick and wounded soldiers, probably in the same way they had ceased to attend the convention: "But if you will stand on a corner any fine evening, you can see the dear creatures riding on horseback, in perfect *shoals*, each one escorted by some man and eighteen mittens, caring and thinking as much about sick soldiers, as if they were so many sheep."[33]

Domesticity Goes Public: Southern Women and the Secession Crisis

Lisa Tendrich Frank

On May 6, 1861, men, women, and children filled the galleries of the Little Rock State House for the meeting of the state's second secession convention. As A. W. Bishop recalled, "Every nook and corner was occupied. The aisles were full—the galleries crowded—men jostled ladies, and ladies each other. Boys perched upon window sills, and nestled by the chairs of members."[1] The onlookers anxiously awaited the convention's final vote on secession, most hoping for disunion and others longing to remain loyal to the Union. Although there were no speeches inside of the hall, the excitement and gravity of the situation was clear. This was not genteel theater, it was rough and tumble politics, and everyone understood the ramifications of secession. When the vote ended, four of the five dissenting voices were convinced to change their votes so that "the wires [can] carry the news to all the world that Arkansas stands as a unit against coercion."[2] When Isaac Murphy announced he would be the lone holdout, the only voice for the Union, the crowd of onlookers erupted. Verbal threats filled the room, as men and women hissed at the decision. As the threats of violence grew louder, a wealthy and prominent widow took center stage. After watching the entire drama unfold, Martha Trapnall tossed her bouquet at Murphy's feet as a sign of moral support for his position.

Trapnall's public and highly political statement was a particular form of gendered speech, one that many women had used and perfected in earlier years. Through these and other acts, the voices of women who were often unwilling or unable to make public speeches entered the public sphere. During Arkansas's first and more contentious debate over secession a few months earlier, women routinely threw flowers at the feet of their beloved speakers. Some supported secession, and others threw flowers at the Unionist majority. In this earlier context, flowers provided a means for women to make their individual voices heard in a setting that only formally acknowledged the voices of men. Unlike the communal cheers and hisses that also accompanied the earlier speeches, the tossing of flowers was an individualistic act, one that brought the identity of the flower-tosser into the public discourse. When the second secession convention met, the near unanimity regarding secession eliminated the necessity for speeches. Consequently, the tossing of flowers for favored politicians was not routine during the second secession convention. In fact, the votes were cast without public discussion until near the end of the process when Chairman David Walker pleaded with the dissenters to change their minds to allow the state to present a unified front on the issue. Walker's speech opened the door for Murphy to voice his view. Murphy subsequently insisted that he made his vote after "mature reflection ... and I cannot conscientiously change it." Murphy's speech, in turn, opened the door for Trapnall to voice her own cautionary concerns about disunion. Her tossing of flowers, in essence, seconded his vote and reminded the audience that even the most respected members of society were divided. In addition, it provided Murphy with the moral backing of white womanhood. Although they hissed at her gesture, no members of the audience were willing to cross the line that Trapnall's symbolic defense provided. After all, many members of the audience, as well as white Southerners across the newly forming Confederacy, declared secession a necessary step to protect a Southern way of life that gloried in the sanctity of white womanhood as much as it defended the institution of slavery.

Trapnall, the dignified widow of a prominent lawyer and merchant, clearly qualified as a Southern lady. The mob cooled its personal rhetoric and instead set its sights on the hated Yankees and the prospect of war.

Although the presence of women at Arkansas's and other states' secession conventions comes as no surprise to many people, women's active involvement in the politics of secession and Civil War may. Before the Civil War, most Americans would have agreed with Margaret Mitchell's narrator in *Gone with the Wind* who asserted that war "is men's business, not ladies'."[3] However, as Southern states debated disunion, seceded, prepared for war, and sent men off to fight the Yankees, many white Southern women demonstrated that the Civil War *was* their business. Their participation in these highly politicized events became essential to the Southern war effort in its infancy and its continuation. White women's roles in the war, noted by many writers and scholars in the years that followed, were not merely ornamental. Women did not simply support their men or blindly follow their state and region into war. Instead, white Southern women shaped the public discourse as they provided and withdrew their support on their own terms.

White women in antebellum America did not have access to ballots, so in essence they voted with their actions. Women, who had entered the realm of politics in varying forms in previous years, used their influence and abilities to push the men of their families to act in the political realm during the sectional crisis. White women around the South filled the galleries of secession debates, wore ribbons and other accessories to proclaim their loyalties, wrote editorials and letters in support of their positions, and otherwise demonstrated their political acumen in the 1850s and early 1860s. In these ways, white women engaged in and expanded the political sphere in order to actively participate in it. During the secession crisis, women of all classes, who could not exert their influence or express their political opinions through voting, nevertheless acted in ways that clearly demonstrated their involvement in politics. They made themselves essential to the war effort as they brought their domestic roles into the public sphere. Without the support of Southern women, the Confederacy could not have waged the war that it did. Women provided the uniforms, food, and other necessities for Southern soldiers. In addition, they worked as unofficial recruiting officers, sent letters of encouragement to men at the front, and maintained the homefront so that their menfolk did not have to worry about business at home. They transformed their domestic activities, bringing their skills into the political and public realm as they worked for the Confederacy.

War and politics were not the only activities considered "men's business" in antebellum America. Most public endeavors fell under this heading. During the nineteenth century, women's lives grew more and more focused around and circumscribed by the home and what were deemed domestic chores. Although some scholars have overstated the rigidity of the boundaries of behavior as well as the extent to which the spheres were separate, most acknowledge that the concepts of feminine space and roles were repeatedly defined and redefined in antebellum America. Within this context, both Southern and Northern women used assumptions about femininity to their advantage in order to participate in the public domain. Throughout the nineteenth century, women took on roles—often those of teachers, writers, and reformers—that played on public notions of "feminine" qualities.[4] The rise of a middle class and the separation of the workplace from the home further gendered people's conceptions of place and role. Women, who had previously taken an active, if unrecognized, role in the support of their families, became relegated to the home and its domestic chores as their husbands went off to work.[5] As a result, the "domestic" and "public" spheres became increasingly separate and gendered. The separation of the sexes in both the North and South fueled the ideals of "true womanhood," which stressed piety, purity, submissiveness, and domesticity.[6] Although the idea of separate spheres excluded women from "public" activities, it gave women control over the domestic aspects of their lives. They gained the power to run the household and raise their children as they saw fit. This command over the domestic sphere proved especially true in the white South. As the holders of the keys to all rooms, stores, pantries, and bureaus, elite Southern women controlled the domestic activities of their households. Those chores that they did not do themselves, they directed others, especially domestic slaves, to do for them.[7] Men and women moved between both spheres, often defining the arena by the work being done there at a specific time. Although not always in the public eye, white women constantly participated in public life.[8]

The Civil War and the political crisis that led up to it forced all Americans to reevaluate white women's visible place in society.[9] Rather than follow men into disunion or adhere to their husbands' Unionist sympathies, many white women pushed the men around them to act. These women often became the impetus for votes in favor of or against secession, and they remained involved as the men prepared to march off to battle. In addition, as the war increasingly affected their lives through shortages and the deaths of loved ones, white women willingly reshaped their roles in the South. They became active participants in the battle for Southern nationhood. Women's vocal roles during the sectional crisis and secession continued with the onset of war. In addition to the physical support that they lent to their nation, white Southern women helped to develop and sustain Confederate nationalism.[10] From the outset of the sectional debates and on through the fighting, Confederate women refused to accept a passive role, and they demonstrated their political awareness through their words and actions.

During the decade before secession, white women in Arkansas and elsewhere found themselves increasingly engaged in politics.[11] Although they could not vote or hold office, these women understood that their husbands and fathers were to represent their interests, although indirectly, in public. Therefore, they frequently advised their male representatives, especially husbands, about the political opinions they had formed from their own experiences. For many women, even on the frontier, engaging in politics was unavoidable. As part of their domestic responsibilities, women often attended church in far greater numbers than did men, as they were deemed the moral guardians of Southern communities. As the sectional dispute grew, ministers and preachers increasingly filled their sermons and homilies with political guidance and warnings. Women also increasingly attended political rallies and social gatherings. Women helped develop the growing omnipresence of politics in antebellum life. As scholars of nineteenth-century politics have demonstrated, "partisanship was indeed a consuming passion and pastime for antebellum Americans."[12]

White Southern women's active participation in the public sphere pre-dated the secession crisis. Far from the sheltered, politically ignorant ladies they have often been portrayed as, many Southern women paid close attention to the political events around them and frequently engaged in the political discourse of the day. They attended rallies, formed their own auxiliary political societies, publicly spoke on political issues, and worked for political causes.[13] In addition, they subscribed to party papers, read the news, and discussed it in depth with friends and family of both sexes. These activities increased as sectional tensions flared. One scholar noted that despite claims to the contrary, "everyone knew that the southern ladies followed political events closely, debated them hotly, and often battered their men on the issues."[14] Women may have been formally excluded from the political arena, but in practice they participated in politics constantly.

Women could not participate in the public sphere in the same way that men could; they could not vote, and most residents of Arkansas and the rest of the South would have likely shunned a woman who publicly voiced her opinions about politics directly. However, scholars have recently recognized that during the secession crisis, "male and female secessionists argued that women should be Confederate partisans and should play a public role in promoting the cause of southern independence."[15] For their part, white Southern women found ways to articulate their opinions on secession and war. Rather than being soothing voices of moderation, as many proponents of female suffrage suggested years later, many Southern white women appealed to the other extreme. "During the secession crisis and the war, southerners from Virginia to Texas commented on the political influence of the ladies, which, they said, heavily bolstered the extremists."[16]

Secession, in particular, allowed women an opportunity to demonstrate their political knowledge and assert their political opinions. Although social mores excluded women from the formal debates at the conventions, Unionists and secessionists called upon women's support throughout the South. In addition, many women actively followed and tried to shape the public discourse surrounding sectionalism and, ultimately, secession. They read newspapers, attended political rallies, and listened to the increasingly political sermons of their ministers. This politicized behavior did not represent anything new. After all, part of being an American, male or female, meant to consume and produce ideas about politics and current affairs. The secession debates simply provided a single, and often polarizing, issue for Americans to consider, discuss, and debate. As one scholar has noted, "in the South as a whole, the political mobilization of white women ... culminated ... in active support of the Confederacy by most women and active support of the Union by some."[17]

Privately, many white women had never had difficulty expressing their political opinions. Educated women began keeping extensive journals in the 1850s and 1860s to record what they understood
to be historic events.[18] Within these journals, they discussed the
political issues of the day, described their debates with friends and
family over these issues, and recorded their attendance at political
functions. They also demonstrated their own personal assessments of
current affairs, and even how they differed from those of their
fathers, brothers, and husbands. Although many white women
received some of their news through their male relations, women's
diaries and journals demonstrate their independent political
thought. Some Southern women consciously recognized how the
secession crisis transformed their personal thoughts and writings.
For example, in her journal, Gertrude Thomas noted her new fasci-
nation with the political and war-related events around her:
"Political events have absorbed so much of my Journal to the exclu-
sion of domestic matters that one might readily suppose that I was
not the happy mother of our darling children."[19] Like Thomas, many
white women could not remain passive or silent now that the stakes
of conversations seemed to have gotten so high. Julia Gardiner Tyler,
wife of former president John Tyler, visited Washington to see the
Peace Conventions because, "everything in the political world is calculated to interest me, and I do not expect or desire gay entertain-
ments under such circumstances as exist."[20] She wanted a first-hand
experience with the political events shaping her life.

Likewise, when the secession crisis came to a head, elite white
Southern women had much to say on the issue. They especially paid
close attention to the contentious presidential election facing the
nation. As the election of 1860 approached, political affairs perme-
ated every part of society. As one slaveholding woman noted, "The
election excitement runs so high, men, women, even children, take
part. The papers are full."[21] This constant glut of news on the elec-

tion was as true in Arkansas as it was elsewhere, as the newspapers divided between Unionist and secessionist stances. The sparring viewpoints in the papers allowed women across the South to form their own opinions about the nation and the crisis it faced.

Proximity to state capitals and secession debates similarly allowed white women the opportunity to make up their own minds about politics and to express those ideas. South Carolinian Leora Sims rejoiced that she lived in her state's capital because she could "go to the Legislature and hear all the speeches." Sims, who hoped that her friend Harriet Palmer's "southern blood is as fiery as mine," professed herself a "regular fire eater."[22] Sims easily adopted the political jargon of the day and eagerly involved herself in the daily debates over secession. In most cases, Southern women acknowledged that the questions facing the nation could split it. Georgian Dolly Lunt Burge assumed that the 1860 election "may be the last presidential Election Our United Country will ever see."[23] White Southern women painstakingly followed the secession debates and then asserted their educated opinions to those around them. Male relations recognized women's thirst for political information and sent detailed accounts of political speeches and news.[24] Furthermore, as self-proclaimed patriotic Southerners, many white women pushed their husbands toward secession after Lincoln won the 1860 presidential election. Unmarried secessionist women similarly used their "availability" to their advantage, refusing to date, let alone marry, a man who did not share their political leanings. By appealing to their husbands' sense of familial duty and honor, elite Southern women further encouraged men to echo their political sentiments and vote for secession.[25]

The politics of slavery and sectionalism also confronted Southern women who traveled, especially to the free states. In 1860, while in New York, one Southern woman encountered a "Wide

Awake" procession for the Republican Party. This evening parade forced her to consider the ramifications of a potential Lincoln victory. Her mind was made up—his election would allow for the disunion for which she already longed. "If the rail-splitter Lincoln and the mulatto Hamlin carry the North, the South will rise as one man and secede from this already detested Union. Never have we had our rights, and never will the North be content until the South submits to be governed by it puritanical, self-righteous, meddlesome self." Later on the trip, she continued to encounter and participate in political talk. On trains, she "heard nothing but the chances of the different candidates discussed, Douglas, Bell and Lincoln." From this she concluded that "if Lincoln is elected, 'twill be because he is the representative of enmity to the South, and not from any appreciation of the North. Lincoln, a course, uncultured back-woodsman, and Hamlin a mulatto! Ugh! it makes me sick to think of it." The political discussion continued throughout her journey. "As we neared home, political talk got stronger, and when the cars stopped at Fort Motte [SC], several young men got on board.... They were 'The Minute Men' ... 'sworn to defend the state.' Then we knew Carolina had her Minute Men ready to meet 'The Wide Awakes' of the hateful North."[26]

As this slaveholding woman had realized from her journey, Americans constantly discussed and debated politics during these contentious times. Sex did not disqualify one from political discussions; women around the nation demonstrated their political loyalties at all opportunities. Often these political views interrupted friendships and social gatherings. For example, Ellen Sherman, wife of United States general William Tecumseh Sherman, informed her mother that St. Louis, Missouri, "is perfectly quiet and seems firmly in the hands of the United States authorities." However, the city was not a pleasant place for Sherman to be at the time because "the Secessionists (and indeed all of my acquaintances are Secessionists, now, even the Pattersons) are rampant, and vehemently express their hatred and detestation of the United States Government. There is but little pleasure in visiting as conversation must be constrained or sentiments would jar too rudely."[27]

Southern women, frequently as educated in the history of their nation as their male counterparts, drew upon the rhetoric of the American Revolution in their discussions of secession. Just as they noted that South Carolina had established a company of Minute Men to protect the state from Northern encroachment, men and women around the South drew comparable parallels between their times and Revolutionary ones. White Southern women affirmed their belief in the necessity of their own revolution against what they perceived as Northern aggression. As one white woman insisted, "revolution we must call it, as secession but faintly conveys our idea. We do not claim to have left—our Union, but we do claim to have the right to maintain it.... The North gave up the Constitution long before we did."[28] Women clearly understood the implications of the political events around them and willingly engaged in promoting and debating the ideas of secession.

Across the South, white women debated whether the election of Lincoln was enough of a provocation for a split. One Southern woman explained immediate secession as a necessary choice, insisting that a Lincoln victory would irrevocably destroy the South. "Why, in four years we would have no rights worth fighting for!" she wrote. As a woman, she also worried about the households that would, she claimed, be damaged by Lincoln's success. "We should make a stand for our rights—and a nation fighting for its own homes and liberty cannot be overwhelmed. Our Cause is just and must prevail."[29] She hoped the voting members of her family would agree and make sure her voice was heard.

As citizens in Arkansas pondered whether they would follow the Lower South into the Confederacy, some secessionist women recognized that their future was tied to the rest of the South and its unity on the issue. From Oxford, Mississippi, Kate Thompson kept up on all of the war reports: "If it was not for the war news, I would hardly read the papers." She closely watched the actions of other Southern states, noting that "I like our Flag very much and do not care whether we have any more stars added to it or not (except Arkansas)—we must have her."[30] Thompson may not have cared if the so-called Border States joined the fledgling Confederacy, but she felt that the inclusion of Arkansas was paramount to showing a unified front.

Women throughout the South focused much of their energies on following and influencing the political decisions of their states. Just as women filled the gallery at Arkansas's secession convention, so white women across the South attended the debates in their area and strove to make their voices heard. Margaret Sumner McLean's constant attendance at Virginia's legislative sessions was not unusual. McLean recorded her excitement at attending the Richmond sessions as well as her attention to the details of secession. On January 9, 1861, she observed that, "Mr. [William H.] Seward drew a crowded house to-day. We went at nine o'clock in order to get seats, and found difficulty in obtaining them even at that early hour." She and the other ladies in attendance were not first-time visitors, nor did they all agree on the correct course of action. "We spend so much time in the Senate that many of the ladies take their sewing or crocheting, and all of us who are not absolutely spiritual provide ourselves with a lunch. The gallery of the Senate is the fashionable place of reunion, and before the Senate meets we indulge in conversation—sometimes very spirited, though generally the opposing factions treat each other with great reserve—a very necessary precaution." McLean, like other Southern women, understood the significance of additional states seceding as she commented on Mississippi's recent decision.

"Mississippi secedes, and I suppose the others will follow soon, as it seems to be the policy to 'speed the parting guest.' The tall, handsome, and belligerent Mississippi women in ecstasies, and the children making a Fourth of July of it with firecrackers, etc. I am becoming accustomed to it."[31]

After Southern legislatures voted for secession, many elite white women publicly applauded their states' decisions to leave the Union. For example, as other states began to follow South Carolina's lead, Emma Holmes wrote that she was "doubly proud ... of [her] native state, that she should be the first to arise and shake off the hated chain which linked us with Black Republicans and Abolitionists."[32] Holmes was not alone in her anti-Union sentiments or her willingness to state them. White women across the South longed to join South Carolina and break free from the United States. In January, Anna Maria Cook declared, "I hope before long Georgia will be with South Carolina seceded from the Union."[33] Similarly, Judith McGuire longed for her state to wholeheartedly embrace its secession and "most earnestly hope[d] that the voice of Virginia may give no uncertain sound; that she may leave [the Union] with a shout."[34] When their states finally seceded, many Southern women rejoiced. One proclaimed, "the very name of Georgian is of itself a heritage to boast of. I have always been proud of my native state but never more so than now. Nobly has she responded to the call for troops."[35] Around the South, other women similarly applauded the ultimate secession of their states. Emma Mordecai noted that, "Our dear mother ... is satisfied that her anxious wish for Virginia to secede has been gratified."[36] With these comments, white women demonstrated their commitment to the political changes affecting their lives.

Women around the South justified their participation in the political debates surrounding secession in many ways. For example, Mary Boykin Chesnut claimed her support of secession as a necessary outgrowth of her upbringing. "My father was a South

Carolina Nullifier.... So I was of necessity a rebel born."[37] Others contradicted their families, pushing them in directions that they may not have taken on their own. In all cases, however, white Southern women's political and historical knowledge gave them the confidence both to voice their opinions to the men of their family as well as to know that their husbands, fathers, and brothers would listen to these ideas.

Unionist women also voted with their actions before and after secession. Many Unionist women found comparable ways to support the United States or left the area for a more politically hospitable environment. Perhaps most notably, many white women voiced their concerns about secession publicly in newspapers. Historians have discovered that these actions occurred throughout the South: "Even in the arch-conservative Deep South, white women often ventured into the male-dominated public world. Their actions denied the fictional rigidity of separate spheres, blurring the line between public and private that antebellum Americans never quite fixed, despite the rhetorical support it constantly received."[38]

Once Southern states seceded, white women continued to act on their political leanings, and their leanings were diverse. Although some white women vehemently supported the fledgling Confederacy, others maintained their loyalty to the United States. In either case, women did everything in their power to support their nation and its war effort, often bringing their domestic roles into the political and public realm. Like other women throughout the North and South, Arkansas ladies joined the war effort by starting aid societies. These groups of white women gathered in private homes, churches, and public buildings to make flags, clothes, and other items for the soldiers. Their work ensured that the men, at least in the war's early stage, would have necessities such as uniforms, socks, and blankets as they headed off to face the Union soldiers. Women's enthusiasm for the Confederate war effort inspired them to begin these endeavors immediately and sometimes even ahead of secession. For example, in anticipation of the impending secession vote, women in Camden began a sewing society two weeks before Arkansas officially seceded from the Union. If their communities would not yet take up the fight, they would initiate the process. Their efforts were greatly appreciated by the men of the community, who marched to war well-dressed in the garments provided by these women. In addition, soon after secession, Little Rock's Theatre Hall became a manufacturing plant. Each day, volunteer women working there made seventy-five pairs of pants and 200 jackets for Confederate soldiers. This mobilization was almost immediate. Only six weeks after secession, the *Weekly Arkansas Gazette* [Little Rock] reported that volunteer women "have made nearly or quite three thousand military suits, upwards of fifteen hundred haversacks, and probably five thousand shirts, and have also covered over twelve hundred canteens." The article also marveled at the willingness of the women to perform these tasks "so cheerfully and so faithfully.... They are willing to labor on and to the end with a high and holy purpose."[39]

In addition to supplying the troops with clothes and food, members of local societies also made flags for newly forming Confederate regiments. These activities, done alone or as a group, allowed women the opportunity to assert their political opinions as well as demonstrate their support for the soldiers. For example, Searcy, Arkansas, women presented the local Yellow Jacket company with a flag inscribed "No Backing Out." In this and other instances, Southern women literally stitched their way into the political sphere.[40]

Not all flags offered such a clearly stated message, although all were imbued with the political aims of the women who made them. Across the South, women's groups made flags and held elaborate presentation ceremonies for departing regiments. Both were

The women of Paraclifta, Arkansas, reportedly made this Confederate flag for the 22nd/35th Arkansas Infantry Regiment. In addition to creating flags for departing soldiers, women also made clothing and other supplies for Southern troops. Courtesy of the Old State House Museum, Little Rock.

designed to inspire men as they headed off to battle. Reading the words provided for her by a local preacher, Miss Whitney at Des Arc reminded the departing soldiers that "the liberties of all future generations stand suspended in doubtful poise, and you must go forth and contend for the prize." She acknowledged the difficult task the men faced in leaving loved ones behind, noting that, "'Tis true that the tears and sobs of an aged mother ... the trembling accents of a loving wife and darling sisters, are enough to wring drops of blood from the heart that is not steel." However, she reminded them that they faced an important task and "no wailings, no cries are equal to those of expiring liberty as she lies prostrate, bleeding at every pore." Whitney concluded with language designed to remind the soldiers of women's support of their battlefield roles. "In behalf of the ladies of

46

West Point, I present to you this banner wrought by their own hands. When marshaled before the booming cannon and exposed to the solid sheets of liquid death, may it inspire your souls and nerve your arms and lend new courage to your drooping spirits."[41] The flag presentation ceremony also included a speech by the commanding officer receiving the banner. He recognized women's roles in inspiring soldiers to fight for the Confederacy: "And while battling for our rights under this banner, we will call to mind the donors of this beautiful flag, who are far away from us, like angels of mercy, sending up their war prayers for our success. Again ladies, we bid you a farewell, hoping God will protect you at home while we defend you abroad."[42] The flags that women across the Confederacy presented to their soldiers demonstrated not only women's support of the men heading off to battle, but also their desire to remind those men of the need for their military service. In essence, the flags became an emblem of women's political interests; the men fought, in part, to represent their women at home.

Dedication to the political meanings of secession also came across in daily acts of individual women. Southern women displayed their support of secession and war by cheering on and providing for the soldiers as they left for battle. As one soldier noted, "The ladies would come out at every house and crossroads to give us their smiles, and they brought bouquets of flowers of the sweetest fragrance, fruit of the rarest and richest quality to distribute and also buckets of cool fresh water. We received nice vegetables, fruit, melons, and cakes that were adorned with roses and evergreens."[43] These actions let departing soldiers know that women approved of secession and the war against the Union.

Elite women's political participation in secession may have been restricted to words and symbolic acts, but their roles in the public realm grew when men moved to the battlefield to exchange gunfire rather than insults. This development gave Confederate women across the South increased reason to follow politics. With their futures explicitly tied to the war, and as their sons, husbands, and fathers risked their lives for the Confederacy, women became even more voracious partisans. Their early celebration of Confederate military success would ultimately lead to more concrete support of the Southern war effort. Drucilla Wray, like others, celebrated the capture of Fort Sumter after the first shots were fired in what would become a lengthy war. "I have just heard that Fort Sumpter is in possession of the Confederate States, Hurrah for Carolina!!! and her noble sons."[44]

The political passion of female Confederates led many men to boast about the bravado of their women. Bragging about the ease with which Southerners could defeat Northerners—one man even "asserted that Mr. Travis's school girls could defend Searcy."[45] At the same time, the exalted position of white women in the South proved a great motivator for white men on the battlefield. Henry Morton Stanley recalled that "even women and children cried for war," and their calls were more impassioned than those of the men. "Inflamed as the men and youths were, the warlike fire that burned within their breasts was as nothing to the intense heat that glowed within the bosoms of the women. No suggestion of compromise was possible in their presence." Southern women's stance on the issue influenced men's decisions to enlist and fight. As Stanley noted, "If every man did not hasten to the battle, they [women] vowed they would themselves rush out and meet the Yankee vandals. In a land where women are worshipped by the men, such language made them war-mad."[46]

Women recognized their importance in inspiring the men to fight for the Confederacy. Once the hostilities began, white Southern women made themselves essential to the Confederate war effort by encouraging men to enlist. In this endeavor they drew upon the power of their femininity and cast their own votes in favor of secession and the war. Across the Confederacy, women used their feminine wiles to entice men into service. Women taunted, cajoled, and shamed men into eventually joining the Confederate forces. Stories abound about women who refused to marry, or even talk to, any man who did not support the Southern war effort by enlisting. These women's actions appealed to the manhood and honor of white Southern men and urged them to fill the ranks of the military because, as Mrs. Allen S. Izard asserted, "I

Seventeen-year-old Henry Morton Stanley, initially uninterested in enlisting in the Confederate army, joined the "Dixie Grays" after receiving a box full of feminine undergarments. From The Autobiography of Sir Henry Morton Stanley *(New York: Houghton Mifflin, 1909).*

sh[oul]d hate a man who w[oul]d flinch, even f[ro]m martyrdom for his Country."[47] Men who refused to enlist often found themselves snubbed by the ladies. Emma Edmonds, a Union spy born in Canada, agreed with a soldier who told her that Southern women were "the best recruiting officers," refusing "to tolerate, or admit to their society any young man who refuses to enlist."[48]

In addition, in several instances, women sent petticoats to men who did not immediately enlist, humiliating these men into the Confederate forces. Henry Morton Stanley was sent "a chemise and petticoat, such as a negro lady's-maid might wear." Stanley "hastily hid it from view, and retired to the back room, that [his] burning cheeks might not betray [him]." Later that day, when asked, "if I did not intend to join the valiant children of Arkansas to fight," Stanley replied in the affirmative.[49] He would rather put his life on the line for the Confederacy than have to deal with the wrath of his female neighbors. The woman's message had certainly been heard and its implications understood. Similarly, a woman in Selma, Alabama, reportedly broke off her engagement to a man who did not enlist. She sent him a petticoat, a skirt, and a note reading "wear these, or volunteer."[50]

As the war continued, white Southern women continually demonstrated their willingness to take their domestic roles public. Many increasingly, and willingly, participated in public life by taking on government jobs, running farms and plantations, nursing wounded soldiers, becoming spies, enlisting as soldiers, and raising money for Confederate soldiers. In all of these endeavors, women displayed their political allegiances, often making personal sacrifices for the Confederate cause.

In conclusion, Margaret Mitchell's assertion that war "is men's business, not ladies'" falsely characterized the importance of women to the Civil War in ways that were common in the late nineteenth and early twentieth centuries.[51] It is in this realm of remembering and forgetting that the political importance of white Southern women has been lost. Post-war writers glorified Confederate women's public roles during the Civil War but minimized the political significance of these roles. Instead of acknowledging women as active political participants, Lost Cause works of literature instead emphasized women's willingness to sacrifice for a cause created and pursued by their men. Similarly, this interpretation asserts that the necessity of wartime pushed women into the public sphere where they adapted to new, but often difficult, conditions. They were passive victims of a war that was foisted upon them. In other words, they chose to "stand by their man." Such an interpretation subtly ignores the political underpinnings of Confederate women's participation in the Southern war effort, and it overlooks the ways in which white women chose their own loyalties and encouraged members of their families to act on their behalf. As a result, it minimizes women's roles in and culpability for the secession crisis as well as in the formation of the Confederacy.

The writing-out of women in the political history of the Civil War occurred in Arkansas in much the same way it occurred throughout the rest of the American South. To understand this process, one needs to look no further than the 1907 *Confederate Women of Arkansas*, a volume published by the United Confederate Veterans that contains the personal histories of dozens of Confederate women.[52] In it, several recurring themes emerge. First, women sacrifice for the cause and are frequently the targets of unjust hostilities. The volume contains many reminiscences of how invading Union troops destroyed their homes while the women could do little but passively watch their society crumble. Second, when women were active, the memoirs emphasize how they remained remarkably feminine. They became nurses so that they could care for their wounded; they formed aid societies in order to raise money and supplies for the troops; they formed sewing circles to make uniforms; and they otherwise used their feminine skills in the name of the war. Finally, the women highlighted are never political agents, and secession is hardly mentioned at all. This rendition of gender and politics became the official history of women and the war, and its legacies continue today.

Why They Fought: Arkansans Go To War, 1861

Carl H. Moneyhon

In the spring and summer of 1861, men from across the South began to move into military camps preparing for war. State authorities accepted the first volunteers for military service shortly after the secession of South Carolina, when many in the South came to believe that a war with the North was inevitable. The rush to the colors quickened following the Battle of Fort Sumter, Lincoln's call for troops to suppress the insurrection, and the increasing determination of the Southern states to resist Lincoln's efforts. Arkansas witnessed the same response as the other new Confederate states. Later Arkansas historians reported a flood of troops, often asserting numbers of volunteers far beyond the military-aged population present locally when the war broke out. The zeal of Arkansas to fight appeared overwhelming, a response that seems to defy explanation, given the Western and frontier, rather than Southern, character of much of Arkansas. Ultimately, why did these men who seemed to have so little at stake in the sectional issues that dominated politics during the 1850s and so much to gain from remaining in the Union decide to abandon the United States and fight for a nation just born?

Historians have long pondered the motives of the men who joined the Confederate army in 1861, or the men who joined any army for that matter. That question has become an integral part of one of the most hotly debated issues in Civil War history—that is, why men fight, and, tangentially, what are the very causes of the war. John A. Lynn's influential study of the motivation of French Revolutionary armies published in 1984 was particularly important in establishing the basic framework within which the question of motivation has been examined. Lynn saw the will to fight as being sustained over time by three different steps in motivational development: initial motivation, or the causes that brought men to the army; combat motivation, or the motives that nerved men to face battle; and sustaining motivation, the forces that allowed men to survive through the challenging conditions of a long war. Of these, initial motivation is critical to the process, for without a general rush to enlist, an army could not come into existence. Defining initial motivation also helps establish the cultural context within which the enlistee's decision is made.[1]

Why did Civil War soldiers decide to join the army? The best-known American scholar who has dealt with this topic is James M. McPherson. His study of combat motivation, *For Cause and Comrades*, published in 1997, begins with a discussion of the motives that caused men to join both the Union and Confederate armies in 1861. He concluded that the initial rush to the colors was part of a *rage militaire* that possessed the men of both sections. What produced such an overwhelming desire to fight? McPherson, looking at the statements of the volunteers, concluded that Civil War soldiers were motivated by patriotism and a sense of doing one's duty, a deed that also brought to the soldier respect, esteem, and honor. McPherson saw duty as a response to a moral dilemma, to a situation that presented the individual with a choice of supporting good or evil, right or wrong. When confronted with such a situation, the soldiers' cultural world, that is, the set of ideas that gave their lives meaning, obligated them to act. They joined the army because their world view obligated them to do their part in defeating evil and bringing the conflict to a just or righteous outcome.[2]

While McPherson emphasized the initial ideological motives of Civil War soldiers, ever the cautious historian, he did recognize that every soldier did not fit conveniently into his generalization.

He also acknowledged a basic criticism of his methodology. Some historians have suggested that the statements McPherson relied on cannot be taken at face value. Historian James McCaffrey has been particularly skeptical of this approach to the problem of individual motivation. His study of Mexican War soldiers argues that volunteers in that war often masked their real reason for fighting—a desire for personal glory—with the rhetoric of patriotism and duty. Despite recognizing both the anomalous cases and the criticism of his use of evidence, McPherson largely dismissed this line of reasoning. Admitting that McCaffrey's concern may apply to the writings of Civil War soldiers, he discounted it with the observation, "It is not clear how he knows this." McPherson's support for his own position, however, ultimately rests on his own leap of faith. He notes, "It is impossible to understand how the huge volunteer armies of the Civil War could have come into existence and sustained such heavy casualties over four years unless many of these volunteers really meant what they said about a willingness to die for the cause."[3]

The existence of men whose motives were not ideological and the basic issue of evidence unfortunately leave the central question advanced here—Why did men fight?—up in the air. Is it possible to generalize with greater certainty about the motives of men who went to war in 1861? The soldiers of Arkansas offer a unique group of men with which to test McPherson's conclusions and further explore the question of motivation. As a relatively recently settled state, one would expect concerns with sectional issues to be less important in Arkansas, with the state's soldiers being motivated to a greater degree by other stimuli. The state had become a part of the Union only in 1836, and its rapid economic growth and integration into the rest of the national economy did not get under way fully until the 1850s. Arkansas was a slave state, but its economy hardly resembled those of the other slave states of the South. While the plantation system had grown and come to dominate the economies of some of the state's counties along the Arkansas, Mississippi, and Ouachita rivers, the economic interests of many Arkansans looked to the west into Indian Territory, to the north into Missouri, or toward the northeast where merchants sought the means to break the power of New Orleans over their lives. Many saw the federal government as a benevolent force that they hoped would better their futures, especially by facilitating the construction of railroads. Nonetheless, Arkansans responded to the crisis of 1861 in large numbers, joining units raised across the state to fight for the Confederacy. Did the men who joined do so for the reasons suggested by McPherson, because they saw a moral crisis that demanded they do their duty? Did other forces play a more important role? The state's political and economic situation, different from much of the rest of the South's, offers the possibility for a different view of the forces pushing men to join the Confederate army.

A variety of sources offer insights into the question of motivation. Traditional literary materials used by McPherson have been the most common avenue into the question and remain a critical place to begin. Even in Arkansas, a relatively literate soldiery left numerous letters, diaries, and memoirs that document their military service and often provide statements of the motives of their authors. Despite the possibility that Arkansans might not have the same stake in a war as others in the South, any exploration of these sources indicates that Arkansas soldiers explained their decision to go to arms in much the same terms used by their contemporaries across the South. They felt a moral obligation to become soldiers.

When Arkansas soldiers shared their thoughts concerning their decision to join the army, almost all of them in some way or another identified one central underlying urge. They enlisted because they saw the war as presenting them with a moral dilemma. That dilemma imposed upon them the sense that they were obliged to perform a duty. The sense of duty emerged from various sources, but soldiers usually indicated that their sense of commitment derived from one or a combination of three major cultural institutions. These were ideas of responsibility that came from the ideologies that grew out of their religion, their sense of citizenship, or their concept of family. An officer with the Second Arkansas Mounted Rifles offered a statement typical of others concerning the role of duty when he wrote to his girlfriend in the spring of 1862. James Williamson complained of camp life and his great desire to be back home. In the end, he admitted that he could not bring himself to leave, however. "Duty," he wrote, "seems to call on me to remain where I am."[4]

While most soldiers explained their action in terms of duty, they were much less clear about the character of the moral challenge that required them to act. Some soldiers were very clear about their belief that the crisis had been provoked by the North and that secession and war had become necessary to protect Southern rights and liberties from an abolitionist North that wished to destroy them. They usually failed to explain exactly what rights and liberties were threatened, but they unquestionably believed that the threat was present and duty demanded their service. Stephen T. Fair of Benton County, a member of the Second Cherokee Regiment, provided a typical explanation of this sort when he wrote to his wife shortly after the Battle of Wilson's Creek in August 1861. In that letter, he defined the enemy that he had fought and his own purpose in being in the army. The defeated foe was an enemy of "Southern rights."[5] William E. Bevens, who joined the Jackson Guards, which became Company G, First Arkansas Infantry, provided a similar assessment of what had driven men to war, although it appeared in a memoir written more than fifty years after the war. To Bevens, the rush to arms had been universal as "plantation-owners, lawyers, doctors, druggists, merchants,—the whole South rose as one man to defend its rights."[6]

For other soldiers, the crisis was not the need to protect Southern rights and liberties but the necessity of defending the newborn Confederacy, with soldiers often seeing the war as an assertion of the South's peculiar nationalism. These men had readily transferred their ideas of loyalty to the nation from the United States to the Confederacy. Alex E. Spence explained it this way in a letter to his sister back home in Arkadelphia, written shortly before he left Little Rock for Virginia with the First Arkansas: "You need not look for me home as long as I have an arm to strike for the 'Southern Confederacy' should she need my Services." In fact, he was willing to die for the cause, writing, "I expect the most of us have seen Arkadelphia and its inhabitants perhaps for the last time."[7] William Wakefield Garner of Van Buren offered similar sentiments in a letter written to his sister in the autumn of 1861 and justifying the death of her son from one of the many illnesses that ravaged military camps during the war. He urged her not to grieve because her son had done his duty. "Your boy is gone, he has fallen," he explained, "but honor to his name. It was in a good and righteous cause in defending his country from the ravages of a relentless foe."[8] W. L. Gammage, a surgeon with the Fourth Arkansas Infantry who authored in 1864 one of the first memoirs from the war, summed up his view of the motivation of those men who vied with each other to organize the army when he wrote that they desired to "sustain our new government."[9] Another young Arkansan remembered that when the war broke out, "a good many men in their thirties and boys in their teens were anxious to be enlisted in some company to protect the Confederate states."[10]

A more common motive than either a defense of Southern rights or the fighting for the Confederacy was the decision to fight as a response to the threat the North presented to one's family and local community. Many believed that a Northern victory would somehow enslave the people of the South and their families. Benjamin F. Boone, a member of one of the state units recruited in the summer of 1861, wrote to his wife on the eve of his departure from his training camp to join General Ben McCulloch's army south of Springfield, offering a justification of what might be the loss of his life in battle. This shows how the sense of obligation could often emerge from several sources. While he warned that might die, he did not believe his death would be a pointless one. He explained to his wife that, should he fall, she was to remember, "it will be for your and our childrens liberty and the freedom of our country" that he fought. Such a cause was "holy and just." Clearly it was his duty to fight and possibly die in such a situation.[11]

Strengthening the idea of duty was the belief held by many that if men carried out their responsibilities, they would produce a triumph of a social and moral good. On the other hand, at least some soldiers also perceived that their actions might enhance their position, particularly bringing about public recognition that attached honor to themselves and their family. Honor gave the soldier distinction and ultimately greater status in his community. Lewis Butler of the Third Arkansas Infantry wrote from Virginia in August 1861 of his hopes that the Confederates would conquer the enemy on the field of battle. He worried about death and asked for his sister's prayers to lead him safely through battle. If he survived, however, he believed that victory and his own contribution to that outcome would allow him to return to Arkansas "with honor."[14] G. T. Whisemate, a Searcy resident in the Seventh Infantry, wrote to his wife from Pocahontas in July 1861 in a similar vein, informing her of his life in camp, expressing his fears, but also expressing his personal hopes for what the war would bring to him. Like Butler, Whisemate feared that he might die, but if he did not, he believed he would bring home "with me a name of honor that will never die for I will not back from the danger."[15]

An exploration of traditional sources shows that the men of Arkansas attributed the same kinds of motives to their enlistment as their peers elsewhere in the South used to explain their own actions. The majority of men explained their behavior as being driven by patriotism, by a sense of duty, or by the hope for honor within their community. So is McPherson right about the influences at work in the Confederacy and in Arkansas in 1861? One might ask of Arkansas troops the same question McCaffrey posed in his Mexican War study: How can we know that in their letters home they are revealing their true feelings? It is possible that this question may be answered by looking beyond the reasons that they gave. Does other evidence provide further insight into the motives of the volunteers of 1861? One approach is to examine the characteristics of these men, asking who they were and if they shared anything in common that could offer clues to their motivations.

We actually know relatively little about the characteristics of the soldiers of 1861. Fortunately, it is possible to determine with some degree of accuracy who volunteered. Service records of Arkansas regiments offer relatively accurate lists of the men who were in the Confederate army, including such information as the time of their enlistment and age. Finding these same men in census records and tax rolls adds even more detail to their personal identity, allowing their economic situations and social qualities to be distinguished. Correlating the names in the service records with those in other public records is not always an easy task. Names are misspelled and families were not counted. Still, the fact that service records provide the age of volunteers and where their companies were recruited helps in more accurately connecting these sources and the information they provide. What does such information tell us about why these men may have joined the Confederate army? Does it confirm or refute the motives that they offered for their decision in their letters, diaries, and memoirs?

An examination of a sample of Arkansas companies that were raised in the spring and summer of 1861 provides the kind of information necessary to create a fuller picture of the Arkansas volunteer. The sample consists of four companies, chosen for the time of their enlistment but also for the variety of communities from which they came. The first of these units was Co. A, Sixth Arkansas Infantry, the "Capital Guards," organized at Little Rock by Captain John G. Fletcher and centered around one of Pulaski County's antebellum militia companies. The second was Company C of the Sixth, the "Dallas Rifles," brought to Little Rock from Dallas County to be mustered in by Captain Foster J. Cameron. The third also came from the Sixth, Company E or the "Dixie Grays," captained by Sam Smith who recruited his company in Arkansas County. The final unit was Co. A, Seventh Arkansas Infantry, recruited in June 1861 by Captain Joseph Martin from Randolph County.

These companies were chosen as samples despite the fact that three of them come from the same regiment because they were among the first to be organized at the outbreak of the war. They also represented a good sample of the diversity of Arkansas's society and geography at the time. In 1860, Pulaski County was a community of small farms and some plantations, but with the presence of Little Rock, it also represented the closest thing to an urbanized population in the state. Despite the presence of plantation slavery, only thirty percent of the population was slaves. Arkansas County, on the other hand, was as close to a traditional plantation county as could be found. Its farms and plantations produced crops valued at more than five million dollars in 1860, twice as much as Pulaski County, and nearly fifty-six percent of its population was slave. Dallas County presented a more complex economic picture, with some plantations along the Ouachita River bottoms, but smaller farms dominating the land away from the river. The value of the crops on these farms was less than twenty percent of that of Arkansas County, and only twenty-eight percent of the population was slave. Finally, Randolph County had some farms, but many were of a subsistence character. Much of the land was covered with timber that remained until the postwar years to be developed. In 1860, the value of Randolph County farm products was even less than Dallas County, and only six percent of its population was slave.[16]

Of the more than four hundred men in these four units, there are few letters or diaries that provide much information on their individual motives for enlisting in the army. The fact, however, that later chroniclers of the war in these counties indicated that their people, at least for the most part, were wholeheartedly in support of the Confederacy suggests that the same forces probably were at work within them as elsewhere.[17] Similar influences should have produced comparable motives as those expressed by other Arkansans. If the motives were much the same, then the volunteers for the four companies would have given reasons for their enlistment that resembled those already seen. Did these men share characteristics despite the differences in the communities from which they came? Did they somehow share a set of cultural values that overrode the differences among them that demanded that they go to war? The search for something common among these volunteers must first of all take into account the striking fact that they actually shared few characteristics. The heterogeneity of the men in the companies and regiments organized in the spring and summer of 1861 is remarkable.

The differences within the military companies begin with the very origins of the men in them. Historians often have assumed that these military companies reflected the communities that gave them their names. In fact, in the case of the four companies examined, only one had a majority of men from the county in which the unit originally organized. Dallas County provided fifty-one percent of the men in the "Dallas Rifles." Only forty-three percent of the men of the "Capital Guards" and "Martin's Company" actually came from the counties in which they were raised. The "Dixie

Grays" had the smallest number of local residents—only twenty-nine percent of the men in the company were from Arkansas County. Who were the rest of the men? They came from all over, some not even from Arkansas. Time passed between when captains originally enrolled their companies and when regiments were formed. To fill up their units to full company strength, officers ultimately accepted almost anyone into Confederate service. New men joined almost everywhere, from where the companies first organized, along the march to their point of muster, and in their training camps. An author writing about the character of companies formed at Little Rock recognized this when he wrote, "this being the capital of the State, it is to be presumed that the companies organized here were recruited to some extent from adjoining counties."[18]

Even those men who came from the counties where these units were formed hardly presented a picture of homogeneity. Their occupations represented one mark of their diversity. The men of the "Dallas Rifles" came primarily from occupations connected with farming, but not all were farm owners. Landless common laborers constituted the largest single group in the company with sixty-four percent of men coming from that group. Eighteen percent were farmers or the sons of farmers. Another eighteen percent came from the small towns of the county, listing themselves as professionals, merchants, clerks, or craftsmen. The "Dixie Grays" presented a similar diverse pattern, with forty-one percent of the total listing themselves as laborers. Men classified as farmers made up another twenty-two percent and overseers another fourteen percent. The remaining twenty-three percent included a few professionals, merchants, clerks, a student, and one individual listing himself as a gentleman. In "Martin's Company," all but eleven percent were farmers. The "Capital Guards" differed the most in its constitution from the other three. Craftsmen made up the largest occupational group, at twenty-seven percent. Twenty-four percent of the company were clerks, and twenty-one percent were merchants. Only one percent came from among common laborers, and the remaining twenty-seven percent consisted of a student, an orphan, and farmers and farm laborers.

Ownership of slaves also provides a marker of status within antebellum communities, and, again, the background of recruits differed greatly. Dallas County's recruits came even more heavily from families with vested interests in slavery that would have been expected given slave ownership there. Thirty-six percent of the "Dallas Rifles" either owned slaves or came from slave-owning households, while in the county, only twenty-nine percent of households owned slaves. In Arkansas County, thirty-five percent of families owned slaves, and the same percentage of enlistees were either slave owners or in families with slaves. In Randolph County, none of the men who enlisted were slaveowners. Pulaski County's "Capital Guards," with most of the recruits coming from the town rather than the surrounding countryside, presented the greatest contrast with the surrounding community. While twenty-six percent of the county's households had slaves, only eight percent of the Guards had any direct connection with slave ownership.

The diverse backgrounds of the soldiers of 1861 were apparent not only in any statistical analysis but also to the men themselves. The soldiers recognized the diversity of social classes among their fellow soldiers, a diversity that they often perceived in terms of cultural values. Henry Morton Stanley, who enlisted in the "Dixie Grays" at the age of 17, believed that his own company possessed some similarity of character, but he saw his regiment as consisting of men from much more varied backgrounds. In the case of his own company, he believed it to be a "choice one" when "compared with many others." What made them "choice" in his view was the existence of what he called the "leaven of gentlehood," which reflected the possession of a common value system. He doubted that less than a fifth of the regiment possessed such attributes, however. The remainder were "rough and untaught soldiers" whom he feared were "apt to be perverting in time."[19]

Stanley's assessment was similar to that of men in units raised across Arkansas who perceived that many of their fellow soldiers were little like them. W. J. Peel of the Sixteenth Arkansas found the army in the northwest to be filled with men he called vagabonds, whom he believed "only serve to give an army a bad name and really do no good."[20] George Woosley of the Twenty-fourth Arkansas recognized the same cultural differences in religious terms, when he complained to his wife of the challenges men in camp presented to his values. "It takes a man with firmness," he wrote, "to live in camp a christan [*sic*] life."[21] Surgeon Junius Bragg of Camden recognized many of the same intense cultural divisions among the men in camp when he informed his mother, "I presume there is no situation in which a man can be placed, so well calculated to corrupt and ruin him morally, as living in a camp."[22] Elliott H. Fletcher, a planter from Mill Bayou, was more explicit in his warning to his soldier son that he would find men not only of inferior moral status but also of a lower class. "You and I, my dear son, are both too exclusive and aristocratic in our personal tastes and sentiments for the circumstances that surround us," he counseled. "We must yield somewhat to the inexorable necessities of the caste, or else we incur mortifications."[23]

The same awareness was not always expressed in a negative sense, however. In some cases, soldiers recognized that they were thrown into a world of individual differences in which preconceived notions of social position meant very little. Philip Stephenson of the Thirteenth Arkansas was representative of this type, coming to realize each of his fellows had to be seen as unique and evaluated on their own terms. "The army was a wonderful revealer of character," he wrote, "and even my young eyes learned soon to distinguish and discriminate the differences in men."[24]

A look at just a few of the men who joined these and other companies points up the great diversity among the volunteers of 1861 and the difficulty in determining what brought them together in their common endeavor. Henry Stanley of the Sixth Arkansas, for example, was not even born in the South. Stanley had come to Arkansas from England in the late 1850s and had been working for only a short time at the store in Arkansas County. As a British citizen, he had no obligation whatsoever to serve. In the Sixth, Stanley would serve with Ralph L. Goodrich. Goodrich not only was from the North, he also had only recently arrived in Little Rock while on a trip. A graduate of Hobart College in New York, he was the son of a fairly prominent abolitionist. Equally out of place was Lieutenant Oliver Gray, who helped to organize a company of the Third Arkansas Cavalry. Born in Maine, he had moved to Minnesota as a teen, and had arrived in Dallas County, where he had settled to teach school at Princeton, only just before the war. An Englishman, an abolitionist, and a midwesterner joined up with young men such as Dan Goree of the "Dixie Grays," son of one of Arkansas County's wealthiest physicians and planters, as well as the even more numerous landless laborers of the South. What possibly served as a common motivation for such men? Did these men have any identical traits that would explain their rush to the colors in 1861?[25]

Some common characteristics did appear among the four hundred enlistees in the sample counties. The similarities that did exist suggest the possibility that reasons other than ideological ones prompted their actions. The first characteristic shared by most of these men was their youth. The youngest group, on the whole, were the men of "Martin's Company," in which the average age of the men recruited in 1861 was twenty-one and the oldest man in the company only thirty. The average age of the men of the "Dixie Grays" was twenty-three, although one thirty-seven-year-old man joined, who remained with the unit until the war's end. In the "Dallas Rifles," the average age was twenty-four. The Rifles also included a fifty-year-old and a forty-eight-year-old recruit, but neither of these men survived service beyond the first year of the war. The townsmen of the "Capital Guards" were the oldest, with an average age of twenty-seven, and one man who was forty-one. In fact, the actual ages of the men in these companies may have been even lower, for census figures show some recruits whom the mustering officers listed as eighteen to be much younger. At least five members of the "Dallas Rifles" who were listed as eighteen were younger. The youngest was W. R. Harley, whom the census showed to be thirteen. Two members of the "Dixie Grays" misrepresented their age, including physician's son Dan D. Goree, who was only thirteen. Goree probably came along to fight alongside his four brothers, and no one bothered to contradict his assertion that he was old enough to fight. Three of the Pulaski County recruits fit into the category, the youngest being Frederick Brock, whose actual age in 1861 would have been sixteen.

In addition to their relative youth, possibly an even more important characteristic united many of these men: bachelorhood. Most of these recruits were not married. The unit with the largest number of married men was the "Capital Guards," but still sixty-eight percent of these recruits were not married at the time they enlisted. The other units were composed of even higher numbers of unmarried men. In "Martin's Company," eighty-five percent of the men were not married. Eighty-seven percent of the "Dixie Grays" were not married. The "Dallas Rifles" had the highest number of unmarried men, with ninety-two percent. The great majority of these volunteers were not only young, but they also had few obligations within their communities, few connections to tie them down.

Why, then, did the majority of recruits in 1861 join the army? The backgrounds of the men of the four Arkansas companies examined here present a picture of men who shared few of the characteristics that would account for any well-developed social or political ideas concerning the crisis of 1861. They represented diverse communities, with many men joining companies with men they did not know. They shared little in the way of economic or social identity. The men recognized that their units consisted of men from a wide variety of cultural backgrounds as well. They did, however, share youth and marital status. At least some of the men themselves suggest that it was the latter two attributes that produced their motivation. They came not from some deep-seated patriotic motives, but rather they simply responded to the impulses that govern young men. They wished, in contemporary terms, to "see the elephant," to do something exciting that they had never done before, to fight. When Henry Stanley recalled the motives of his fellow soldiers in the "Dixie Grays," he concluded that there were at least some "passionate patriots" among the men in his company. He believed, however, that most came as the result of other impulses, motivating reasons that included an "appetite for glory, the desire of applause, a fondness for military excitement, or because they were infected with the general craze." He also noted, however, that many came "to avoid tedious toil, or from the wildness of youth." They came because it was the thing that a young, unmarried man would be expected to do.[26]

The testimony of volunteers in other units adds validity to Stanley's observation about the limited role played by political or social ideology among the men of the "Dixie Grays." Among Stanley's other forces, the anxiety to prove one's manhood was frequently one of the individual motives to appear. While American society attributed many different characteristics to manhood, bravery certainly was a major element, and war was an age-old environment to test a man's courage. Most wrote not only of their desire to prove their own courage, but also of their desire to show that they were not the opposite of brave men, to demonstrate that they were not cowards. Sumter Rowland, a young soldier with the Third Arkansas Infantry, wrote a letter from Virginia in the summer of 1861 that expressed his own uncertainty about how he would behave in battle. He hoped, however, to prove that he could act in the right way. "I do not believe I am a coward," he wrote to his sister, "but believe I can face the music." To hurry the test, he insisted that he was "eager for the fray."[27]

Even when the men did not discuss directly their desire to prove themselves as men, it is clear that many in their communities understood the importance this idea played in their society and used it to encourage men to join the army. Lorenzo A. Miers, who joined the Third Arkansas in the summer of 1861, described a recruiting speech he heard that June. When only twelve men stepped forward to sign up, the officer trying to form the company stepped forward and told the rest of the men "he was going to send for lot of hoop skirts & fine bonnets, dress the men up & put them in the parlor." Miers reacted strongly. "I could not stand that," he wrote and then returned to Union County and joined the army. He would later admit, "I went to keep from being called a coward."[28] Henry Stanley provided a similar account of his own entry into the "Dixie Grays." Stanley apparently had no real interest in joining the unit being raised in Arkansas County until he received a parcel, addressed in a feminine hand, that he supposed was some token of regard. Instead he found it to contain a "chemise and petticoat, such as a negro lady's-maid might wear." Embarrassed by the affront, when asked that afternoon if he intended to "join the valiant children of Arkansas to fight," he answered yes.[29]

Other soldiers expressed other non-ideological reasons for their decision to enlist, although these did not appear as frequently. John Lavender of Mount Ida, who joined the "Montgomery Hunters," which became part of the Fourth Arkansas Infantry, was one of these.

In his memoirs, Lavender wrote, "I had always liked to read History of war and always determined to go to a war should the opportunity turn up. Well it turned up."[30] Lavender could not resist the desire to see for himself what war was like and signed up. Some appear simply to have joined for a fight. Indeed, the simple desire for a fight recurs again and again among the writings of soldiers. Ras Stirman of Washington County, another soldier who joined one of the early state regiments in 1861, was typical. In one of his letters, written from northwest Arkansas in July 1861, he reported that the troops were in fine spirits and wanted to fight. He noted that the men were keen for "a chance at the lagger beer Saloons" in Springfield.[31]

Their behavior when they entered the army adds even more support to the idea that many of the recruits of 1861 joined for the excitement the prospective military service offered. They appeared to see military service as something of a lark. Peter Hotze of the Sixth Arkansas recorded in his diary that, while in Little Rock, the men of the regiment were "loud and noisy during the night..., there was a lot of drinking and singing going on and the band played, so that I was quite often awakened from all that noise."[32] Henry Stanley, who camped at Little Rock with Hotze, may have lain awake on the same nights; he also recalled the camp to be filled with singing and drinking throughout the night. He believed that many considered the war to be little more than a summer picnic and all believed it would be over in sixty or ninety days. Few imagined the serious prospects they would face.[33] A soldier from the Second Arkansas Infantry noted a similar lack of seriousness when he reported that the men in his company were "much disposed to do as they pleased," since they consisted largely of "green country boys and young men."[34]

In short, the evidence strongly suggests that few of Arkansas's soldiers volunteered in 1861 because of any sort of ideological consideration. Still, we are confronted with the testimony of so many of them who emphasized patriotic motives for their behavior in their letters home and later in their memoirs. Where did these ideas come from? Possibly, men incorporated them into their attitudes about the war only after they entered the service. Their very decision to enter the army brought them into a world of change that would ultimately alter their very identities. The army provided them with motives that could be used to explain and justify their decision to enlist to their families and friends, explanations that often were not made until the soldier had been in the service for several months. The military of 1861 did not possess the notions of psychology that make it possible to understand the motivation of modern armies, but it did possess the accumulated practical knowledge gained by soldiers from ancient times forward to instill spirit in its men. From their very first day in the army, the men received a constant bombardment of patriotic rhetoric from politicians, officers, and the good people of their communities that explained why they now must fight and die. They heard such speeches as that of Captain Sam Smith of the Grays as he accepted a company flag from the women of Little Rock. Smith thanked the ladies, then addressed his men. "You go as sacrifices upon the altar of your country," he said. "You go with the expectation, and I hope with the heartfelt willingness, to lay down your lives, if necessary, to sustain the honor and reputation of our glorious newly formed Confederacy." His stem-winding speech ended with his admonition: "Let every one be inspired with the determination to take a stand, either to live or die in Dixie."[35]

If the injunctions of their officers were not enough, they faced the likes of Miss Lillian T. Rozelle of Pine Bluff, who told the men of the "Jefferson Guards": "You go, braves ones, to struggle in the dearest cause an American heart has at stake—the rights of this hallowed land of the South! Remember 'it was liberty, not Union, for which our forefathers fought.' ... Let the sacred motto be inscribed on every heart, *'Honi soit qui maly pense,' or 'Evil be to him who evil thinks of it.'*"[36] Here were all of the ideas that soldiers used to explain their absence: duty to secure rights, liberty, the Confederacy, and honor; and, willingness to suffer a noble death if necessary to achieve those ends.

Joining the army for adventure, and then quickly indoctrinated with more patriotic reasons to justify their decision, soldiers would find that neither set of ideas prepared them for what they ultimately encountered. Actual life in the military quickly dispelled any ideas that their service would be a picnic. Doing one's duty would be a serious test. The men of the Sixth Arkansas left Little Rock for Pocahontas, one of the points chosen to concentrate the state's troops for training, on June 19 with drums beating and colors flying, witnessed by a large crowd who went to the river crossing to see them off. Two days later, a private with the "Capital Guards" recorded the impact of the march in his diary. Men had fallen by the wayside, too sick and tired to march. Peter Hotze wrote, "Kremmer got Diarriah, Lincolns feet hurt, Robert Watson had a headache. The whole company was totally exhausted when we arrived at our camp."[37] Henry Stanley described the same march, writing "we had no sooner reached the precincts of the camp than we embraced the ground, pains and aches darting through every tortured limb, feet blistered and bleeding, our backs scorched, and our shoulders inflamed."[38]

Worse was yet to come. At Pocahontas where the Sixth and Seventh mustered into Confederate service, the men experienced an even greater test of their willingness to do their duty: disease. Typhoid fever swept through the camp. Measles followed thereafter. Henry Stanley believed that at least fifty men in the regiment died from "typhus, or malarious fever, aggravated by fatigue and wretched rations."[39] The experience at Pocahontas typified that of men throughout the army. Soldiers with the Third Arkansas in Virginia suffered a similar confrontation with the new realities of camp life, with one of its soldiers writing in August 1861, "The measles have been through our whole regiment and has been fatal to some who taken cold with it and turned to newmonia [*sic*]."[40]

Then these men actually went to war. The Sixth Arkansas fought at Shiloh, where one lieutenant reported that the men went through charge after charge, where they were exposed to the most galling fire, yet fought with the intrepidity of veterans.[41] In the process, however, the "Capital Guards," who went into the fight with only thirty-one effectives. They officially lost only one man, but service records show ten casualties, thirty-two percent of the company's strength. The other companies suffered comparable losses. The Seventh was also there, earning the nickname, "The Bloody Seventh." Decimated in early fighting, the Sixth and Seventh were consolidated in December 1862 and went on to fight in all of the major campaigns of the Army of Tennessee. Few were left of either regiment when the company surrendered in North Carolina on April 26, 1865.[42]

By the spring of 1862, the realities of war challenged all of the ideas that the soldiers may have possessed when they joined. They were involved in a world with little adventure, in which death in the name of a cause was hardly romantic. It was a world of real horror, one that was nothing like the one they had left behind. To sustain themselves in their new world, they now had to learn new rules and find new motives to fight. Private Stanley recalled how everything had changed. "I had to learn that that which was unlawful to a civilian was lawful to the soldier," he wrote. "The 'Thou shalt not' of the Decalogue, was now translated 'Thou shalt.' Thou shalt kill, lie, steal, blaspheme, covet, and hate.... The prohibition to do these things was removed, and indulgence in licence [*sic*] and excess was permissible. My only consolation ... was, that I was an instrument in the strong, forceful grip of circumstance, and could no more free myself than I could fly."[43]

In the military world, few of the rationales that soldiers used to explain their behavior and their lives in 1861 helped give meaning to their new experiences. Indeed, few of them appeared to have gone to war holding any deep political or cultural attitudes about the conflict itself but rather they went to pursue excitement and individual glory. Their leaders, both military and political, quickly gave them ample reasons that allowed them to justify their behavior in patriotic terms. Warfare, however, could hardly be sustained by such motives over the long run. The practical business of waging war would ultimately demand much more to give these men a reason to remain. As suggested by Lynn in his study of the French armies, sustaining combat motivation would have to develop. Arkansas's Confederate soldiers would be forced to find new means to sustain themselves during the next four years of war.

"A Remarkably Strong Union Sentiment": Unionism in Arkansas in 1861

Thomas A. DeBlack

When talking about Unionism in Arkansas in 1861, it is necessary to put that year and the state into a larger historical context. For Unionism in Arkansas, and throughout the South for that matter, was not something that sprang full-blown in 1861. Rather, it rested on a long-standing tradition stretching back to the beginning of the Republic. So perhaps we should begin by noting that no one familiar with the history of the United States in the antebellum era should be surprised by the fact that there was a large reservoir of Union sentiment in the South in 1861. For most of the seventy-two years from the founding of the Republic in 1789 to the outbreak of the Civil War in 1861, Southerners had been the nation's foremost nationalists.

And why shouldn't they have been? They had dominated the national government. As historian James McPherson has noted, "During the first seventy-two years of the republic down to 1861, a slaveholding resident of one of the states that joined the Confederacy had been President of the United States for forty-nine of those years—more than two-thirds of the time. In Congress, twenty-three of the thirty-six speakers of the House and twenty-four of the presidents pro tem of the Senate had been southerners. The Supreme Court always had a southern majority; twenty of the thirty-five justices to 1861 had been appointed from slave states."[1]

Southerners not only dominated the national government, they were in the forefront of those who fought to defend it. The "War

Hawks," those ardent, aggressive young nationalists who lobbied for a second war with Great Britain in the early years of the nineteenth century, were mainly Southerners, including a young Carolinian named John C. Calhoun. When events in that war didn't go well, it was another Southerner, Andrew Jackson, who bailed them out and salvaged the nation's honor with his epic victory at New Orleans in January 1815. Jackson's victory ushered in a wave of nationalist feeling that eventually made him president.

Southerners were also among the nation's foremost nationalists in the Mexican-American War. Many of the men who would later lead Confederate armies played important roles in that conflict. (P. G. T. Beauregard, John Pemberton, James Longstreet, George Pickett, Albert Sydney Johnston, Joseph E. Johnston, Braxton Bragg, and, of course, Robert E. Lee and Jefferson Davis come to mind.)[2]

Perhaps then it is not surprising that, in 1861, Abraham Lincoln overestimated the extent of Southern Unionism and counted on it to head off secession and war. As David Herbert Donald has noted, Lincoln believed that, despite the loud rhetoric of the secessionists, Unionists were a large majority in the South, and given time for tempers to cool, they would be able to defeat the secessionists. He placed great faith in the Old Whig elements in the South and, Donald notes, he "did not believe that any sizable number of rational citizens could contemplate disrupting the best government the world had ever seen."[3]

If Lincoln overestimated the strength of Southern Unionism, many historians and casual observers in subsequent years have underestimated it, seeing a strong thread of secessionist sentiment stretching back to the Virginia and Kentucky Resolutions and proceeding through the South Carolina nullification crisis to Sumter and secession. As William Freehling has demonstrated in *The Road to Disunion: Secessionists at Bay, 1754–1854*, secessionists of any stripe enjoyed almost no success in the years prior to 1854.[4]

Of course, secession did occur, and the war came. What changed? The obvious answer, of course, is that the controversy over the expansion of slavery intensified until it split the two sections apart. There is, however, another way to look at the issue. Historian Alan Brinkley contends that Americans in the mid-nineteenth century liked to believe that the United States was a nation especially ordained by God, and that the Union represented a beacon of liberty and stability that would serve as a model to the rest of the world. But in fact, Brinkley argues, in many ways the United States was not a nation at all but rather a highly decentralized confederation of states with very little in common—states that remained together because the Union was so loose, the central authority of the nation so weak, that differences did not have to be confronted. As the nation began to move in the direction of greater national unity in the 1840s, it encountered major obstacles. Therefore Southerners could afford to be strong champions of the Union, as long as the federal government left them largely alone.[5]

And even if we accept William Freehling's contention that, on the national level, 1854 marked a decisive turning point in the struggle between Southern Unionists and secessionists, Arkansas seems to be out of the mainstream of Southern thought. For even after 1854, antiunionist or disunionist sentiment found very little support among the majority of Arkansans. Now it is true that even as early as the early 1850s, several members of the state's ruling elite, men like Robert Ward Johnson, Thomas Hindman, John Selden Roane, William Sebastian, and Solon Borland, were strong spokesmen for Southern rights.[6] When, in 1850, Johnson issued an "Address to the People of Arkansas," which questioned whether the North and South could remain "under a common government for a period beyond this Congress" and called for "our rights under the Constitution within or without the Union," his appeal fell on deaf ears, and Johnson was forced to do a furious backpedal in order to regain his political viability.[7]

William Woodruff's *Arkansas State Gazette and Democrat* chided Johnson for what it called his "peculiar views" and added, "It is the universal sentiment that the Union must be preserved; and the universal belief is that it cannot be dissolved."[8] A resident of Chicot County, in the heart of the state's cotton-producing region, agreed. In a letter to Woodruff's paper, he proclaimed himself to be a strong supporter of slavery and Southern rights, but also "a Union man" and a friend of compromise. He condemned Johnson's views as "offensive in terms and heretical in principle" and concluded that "[a]s long as the South deals in bombastic declamation in regard to Southern chivalry, disunion, secession, southern confederacy, and all such nonsense, the patriotic, honest men of the free states will not unite with them, and the question will remain unsettled." He added that a tour of the state satisfied him "that Arkansas is still American, altogether American, in hope, thought, and feeling."[9] Whig leader Albert Pike declared that he was "for the Union, the whole Union, and nothing less than the Union."[10]

Events that increasingly polarized the nation seemed to have had little impact in Arkansas. When the bill creating the Kansas and Nebraska territories passed Congress in 1854, a Chicot County planter, writing to renew his subscription to the *New York Weekly Times,* assured the editor that the whole controversy "is a subject rarely ever thought of, or mentioned down here in the midst of the great cotton region of Mississippi.—that there is no interest or feeling in connection with it whatever."[11]

Even the outbreak of fighting there in 1856 did little to change the minds of most Arkansans, despite the fact that Kansas lay less than a hundred miles from Arkansas's northwestern border. A Camden newspaper urged its readers to "Forget about Kansas and rejoice in our glorious wealth, delightful showers, and abundant crops."[12] As late as February 1860, the editor of the *Arkansas Gazette* noted, "[I]t is our belief that the American Union stands on a firmer foundation than ever before. The union of these States is cemented by a community of interest which will forever operate as a natural check to secession or dissolution.... We may assure ourselves that the Union is not in danger."[13]

Why this strong attachment to the Union? Why this seeming dichotomy between Arkansas and many of the other slave states? There are several reasons. Arkansas had just gotten into the Union in 1836, and having been there for less than a quarter of a century it was in no hurry to get out. Beyond that, Arkansas needed the Union more than many other states. Citizens of western Arkansas, bordered by the Indian Territory, wanted the protection and economic benefits that the presence of federal troops supplied. Delta residents hoped to benefit from a federal swamplands reclamation project begun in 1850.[14]

And, of course, as the 1850s progressed and national tensions heightened, Arkansas was experiencing an economic boom unprecedented in its history. By 1860 it would rank 16th of the 33 states in income per capita, a position that it had never occupied before and would never occupy again. Slaveowners accounted for only about 20% of the state's white population, and many Arkansans who did not own slaves saw little reason to ally themselves with a cause they perceived as being little more than an attempt to protect the interest of slaveowners.[15]

Slaveowners themselves were divided on the issue. For while the growing prosperity of the 1850s was general, it was not uniform. The large slaveowners of the southern and eastern lowlands easily outstripped their upland neighbors in prosperity and thus had little reason to want to disrupt a system that seemed to be working very well and promised to get better still. "If cotton will only hold present prices for five years," the *Arkansas State Gazette and*

Democrat noted in May 1857, "Arkansas planters will be as rich as cream a foot thick."[16]

It did not hurt the Union cause in the South that in that same year the Supreme Court handed down the landmark decision in the case of *Dred Scott v. Sandford*, ruling that Congress could not ban slavery from the territories. Even in 1860, as national events increasingly polarized the nation and increased the likelihood of civil war, Arkansans seemed more concerned with the state elections in August that saw the ruling Democratic political dynasty known as the "Family" suffer its first defeat since statehood, at the hands of an insurgent group of Democrats led by Thomas Hindman. The issue of Southern rights and secession played no role in the campaign, and voting patterns in Arkansas showed no great disparity between the uplands and lowlands.[17]

Only with the state elections behind them did Arkansans turn their attention to November's presidential election. Despite the best efforts of many of the state's political leaders, the issues of Southern rights and the protection of slavery had failed to resonate with the majority of Arkansans throughout the preceding decade. The presidential election of 1860 would force Arkansans to confront the issue. Electors for only three of the four candidates appeared on the ballot in Arkansas. The Republican Party's strong stand against the expansion of slavery into the western territories meant that Abraham Lincoln would not be a factor in Arkansas or the rest of the slave South. Of the three remaining candidates, Stephen Douglas, the candidate of the northern wing of the now-sundered Democratic Party, enjoyed the least support in the state. Opposed by both the Family and the Hindman camp, Douglas forces had few newspapers to champion his cause and also lacked the financial resources to sponsor the rallies and barbecues so necessary to political campaigns in the mid-nineteenth century.

The new Constitutional Union Party did have those resources, however. In Arkansas its candidate, John Bell, found great support among former Whigs, including many of the wealthy planters of the southern and eastern parts of the state. John Brown of Camden, a slaveowner, judge, and a former Whig, expressed the sentiments of many Arkansas Unionists. While he remained loyal to the Union, Brown had no sympathy for the party of Lincoln, which he labeled the "Black Republicans." In fact, Brown and many like him seemed to consider the Republicans and the secessionist Democrats as unacceptable poles on the political spectrum. Brown reserved his harshest criticism not for the Republicans but for secessionist Democrats, whom he referred to as "traitorous aspirants for 'rule or ruin' leading the South headlong into destruction!" In his diary, he railed against "Yancy & co., Southern traitors in the name of Breckenridge" and referred to "the Democrats, or rather the Disunionists headed by Traitors of the South." Camden, he noted, was "the strongest opposition community in the state and that is all that reconciles me to the place." The Constitutional Unionists also enjoyed the support of some of the state's more influential newspapers, including the powerful *Arkansas Gazette*, which tried diligently to portray John C. Breckinridge as the candidate of extremism, disunion, and treason.

These aspersions notwithstanding, the final returns in Arkansas showed a clear, if modest, victory for Breckinridge. The Kentuckian received 28,783 votes (53%) to Bell's 20,094 (37%), and Douglas's 5,227 (9%). A quick analysis would seem to indicate that the candidate most associated with Southern rights and disunion garnered 53% of the vote while the two candidates associated with the maintenance of the Union received 46%.

But that analysis is too simple. In fact, it is extremely misleading. As Jack Scroggs pointed out in the *Arkansas Historical Quarterly* in the 1950s and James Woods pointed out in the 1980s, despite the obvious national implications, disunionism had not been an issue in the campaign. Four of the largest cotton-producing counties (Mississippi, Crittenden, Desha, and Chicot) gave sizeable margins to Bell, while many of the counties with the strongest Union sentiment went heavily for Breckenridge.[18]

A more detailed analysis of the vote reveals that Bell did best in those parts of the state where the Whigs had traditionally done well—among the wealthy planters of the Delta and in the business-oriented urban areas, where voters feared a disruption of commerce. Breckinridge ran strongest in the traditionally Democratic northwest and among the farmers and small slaveowners of south and southwest Arkansas who hoped to rise to planter status. It may seem strange that the candidate most identified with slavery and states' rights found such great support in northwest Arkansas, where slavery was least developed. The northwest part of the state had always been staunchly Democratic, however, and the best explanation may be that these voters were more influenced by party loyalty than by the overheated rhetoric about slavery.[19]

In addition to Arkansas, Breckinridge carried all the Deep South and Gulf South states, garnering almost 850,000 popular votes and 72 electoral votes. Douglas received almost 1.4 million popular votes but carried only one state (Missouri) and 12 electoral votes. Bell received almost 600,000 popular votes and carried the border states of Virginia, Kentucky, and Tennessee. None of this was enough to off-set Lincoln's near sweep of the more populous free states. Final national returns gave the Republican candidate more than 1.8 million popular votes and, more importantly, 180 electoral votes. Though he received slightly less than 40% of the total popular vote, his electoral total easily surpassed the total of his three rivals.[20]

In Arkansas, the initial reaction to Lincoln's election was generally mild. On November 17, the *Gazette* editorialized, "Lincoln is elected in the manner prescribed by the law and by the majority prescribed by the Constitution. Let him be inaugurated, let not steps be taken against this administration until he has committed an overt act, which cannot be remedied by law." The editor hoped that the election might spur the growth of a new conservative opposition movement built around the nucleus of the Constitutional Union Party.[21]

Albert Pike also refused to accept Lincoln's election as a cause for breaking up the Union. He hoped rather that it might unify the South around a new sectional party.[22] Even the Family's *True Democrat* announced itself as "opposed to premature agitation or hasty legislation," while the Family-controlled Fayetteville *Arkansian* advised its readers to "wait until after his [Lincoln's] inaugural and see what course he will pursue."[23] Only a few of the more extremist newspapers called for immediate secession. Scroggs contends (correctly, I believe) that even after the election of Lincoln, the majority of the state's citizens remained strongly attached to the Union.[24] Albert Rust, a Family Democrat from El Dorado in Union County, declared that people never had less cause to complain of the government or to threaten its overthrow, that secession was an insult "to wise and patriotic sages who framed the Constitution," and he added, "if the opinions and wishes of nine-tenths of the people of Arkansas, are reflected by her representatives at Little Rock, her course in the present political crisis will be temperate and conservative."[25]

In December, South Carolina announced that it had severed its ties with the Union. This action, coming only six weeks after Lincoln's election and more than two months before his inauguration, caught Arkansas Unionists and even some secessionists by surprise, and it hastened the demise of the old political alignments. On December 21, Senator Robert Ward Johnson and Congressman Hindman, less than a year removed from their near-duel in the nation's capital, collaborated on a joint statement calling for a state convention to consider secession.[26]

The fact that a state had actually seceded hastened the political realignment in Arkansas. Even before secession, large planters in the southern and eastern lowlands (many of them former Whigs who had supported John Bell in the November election) now joined forces with Democrats to form a common front for secession. Among the yeomen farmers in the upland counties of northern and western Arkansas, however, Unionist sentiment remained strong. Unionists held mass meetings throughout the northwest part of the state, and in some less likely areas as well. The state legislature received anti-secession resolutions from Sebastian, Marion, Carroll, Newton, Searcy, and Van Buren counties. But resolutions also came from Sevier, Clark, Conway, and Pike counties.[27]

On December 22, the state House of Representatives gave in to growing pressure and called for a convention to consider secession, although the more conservative state Senate did not concur until January 15, 1861. By the terms of the measure, voters would go to the polls on February 18 to decide whether or not to call a convention and to elect delegates. As James Woods has noted, Unionist candidates had the unenviable task of asking voters to reject the convention while simultaneously soliciting their votes as delegates to the convention.[28]

The Unionist dilemma was compounded by events of early 1861. Between January 9 and February 1, six more Deep South and Gulf South states left the Union, including the neighboring states of Mississippi, Louisiana, and Texas. The secession of the Deep South states convinced even more Arkansans who had previously stood by the Union and hoped for compromise to go over to the secessionist camp.[29]

Local affairs also contributed to the secession frenzy. In November 1860, Capt. James Totten and sixty-five troops of the

Second U.S. Artillery Regiment had been transferred to the previously unoccupied federal arsenal in Little Rock. The presence of the federal troops had aroused little comment or notice until the following January, when a rumor that the garrison was to be reinforced spread by the newly completed telegraph line from Little Rock to Memphis, then downriver to the secessionist stronghold of Helena. The rumors were baseless, but Helena area firebrands demanded that the governor seize the arsenal and offered the services of five hundred men to accomplish the task.[30]

Such a precipitate and illegal action was too much even for Governor Rector. He replied that while Arkansas was still in the Union the governor of the state had no right to seize federal property. Rector was not content with a clear and unambiguous statement, however. He went on to say that any attempt to reinforce the arsenal would be an act of war. By the time his adjutant-general (who was also his brother-in-law) reworded and released the statement, it appeared that the governor was encouraging a spontaneous action on the part of the people to seize the arsenal. By the end of January, hundreds of "volunteers" from Helena, Pine Bluff, and other delta communities had arrived in the capital, and rumors abounded that many more were on the way.[31]

With the situation threatening to spiral out of control, Captain Gordon Peay, a member of a prominent Little Rock family, called up the "Capital Guards." Historian Calvin Collier has noted that the Guards were composed of "men who represented the legal, medical, banking and business fields of the community and who already were leaders in every phase of political, social and community affairs." In the late 1840s, an earlier incarnation of the Guards had served in the Mexican War, but the current generation was noted mainly for its sponsorship of the picnics and balls that were the highlights of the city's social season.[32]

A staunchly conservative group, the Guards had initially attempted to act as a calming influence between the secessionists and Unionist factions in the capital city until Arkansas decided on what course it would pursue. That level-headed position immediately earned them the enmity and derision of the hot-headed secessionist element that had swarmed into the capital intent on seizing the arsenal by force if necessary. To Governor Rector, however, they were a godsend.[33]

On January 28, the governor called on Captain Totten to peacefully surrender the arsenal on February 7. Totten, the son of a prominent Little Rock physician, was a handsome young man who had quickly become a very popular figure in the capital city's social circles. Outnumbered and "being without instructions from his Government," Totten agreed to the governor's demands, noting that he was "doing what he thought proper and best under all the circumstances, desiring to avoid cause of civil war in this Government, by the first instance of a hostile and bloody collision, yet protesting for himself and in the name of his Government against events beyond his control."[34]

Rector authorized the "Capital Guards" to accept the surrender of the arsenal, and the federal troops evacuated the installation on February 8. The Guards escorted the arsenal's garrison safely through a jeering crowd to the safety of the river at Fletcher's Landing, just downstream from the city. Totten and his men remained in camp at Fletcher's Landing until February 12, when they boarded the steamer *Madora* and proceeded to St. Louis.[35]

On the surface, the bloodless seizure of the arsenal seemed to be a great triumph for the governor and secessionist cause, but many Arkansans disapproved of the action. Little Rock residents were particularly irate at the incursion of large numbers of secessionists into their town and at the actions of the governor. A Pine Bluff resident who came to the city four days after the evacuation of the arsenal admitted that he was "much surprised to find a greatly divided sentiment in relation to the question of secession" and noted that "the Union sentiment prevailed largely at the capital."[36]

Totten also took note of this sentiment in an official report. "It gratifies me beyond measure to be able to bear testimony to the honorable, high-toned, loyal, and law-abiding action taken by the great majority of the most respectable citizens of Little Rock," he wrote to the adjutant-general of the army. "From the richest to the poorest, I am happy to say, there was but one sentiment, and that was in opposition to the course of the governor and those who counseled and aided him in the deed done."[37] Governor Rector was seriously damaged by the affair. Arkansas Unionists denounced him for precipitating a crisis where none existed, and even some secessionists sensed that the governor had lost control of the situation.[38]

Nine days after the evacuation of the arsenal, Arkansans went to the polls to vote on whether to hold a convention to consider secession. (That same day in Montgomery, Alabama, Jefferson Davis of Mississippi took the oath of office as president of the new Confederate States of America.) The election results reflected the ambivalence most Arkansans felt about the issue of secession. An overwhelming majority of Arkansas voters favored the convention (27,412 to 15,826), but the majority of the delegates elected to attend the convention opposed secession. Clearly, while many Arkansans were willing to consider the possibility of secession, most were in no hurry to secede.[39]

On March 4, 1861, Abraham Lincoln assumed the office of president of the United States. In his inaugural address, Lincoln expressed his belief that the union of states was perpetual, and he pledged to enforce the laws and hold federal property. At the same time, he declaimed any intention of interfering with slavery where it already existed. Addressing the South directly, he said, "In *your* hands, my dissatisfied fellow countrymen, and not in *mine*, is the momentous issue of civil war.... With *you*, and not with *me*, is the solemn question of 'Shall it be peace, or a sword?'"[40]

That same day, the Arkansas convention assembled to take up the issue of secession. The make-up of the delegates, like the vote itself, reflected the clear geographic division in the state. Unionists from the northern and western portions of the state enjoyed a narrow majority of the seventy-seven delegates. In a key early vote to select the chairman of the convention, Unionist and former Whig David Walker of Fayetteville narrowly defeated a secessionist candidate by a vote of forty to thirty-five. It was indicative of the course the convention would take. Secessionist delegates gave impassioned speeches, the secessionist press thundered for disunion, delegates from the seceded states of South Carolina and Georgia addressed the convention, Confederate president Jefferson Davis sent his own representative, and both Senator Johnson and Governor Rector made personal appeals. Still the Unionist majority was unmoved. James Woods has noted, "The Unionist-Cooperationist majority never amounted to more than five votes, yet it was enough to control the assembly, and all the major committees were headed by this political party."[41] A disgusted secessionist delegate noted that a "remarkably strong Union sentiment which prevails in this convention, leaves us no hope of the secession of the state of Arkansas from the Federal Union."[42]

After two weeks of intense deliberation, the convention rebuffed every attempt to pass an ordinance of secession or even to allow a popular referendum on the issue. Finally, fearing that southern and eastern Arkansas might attempt to secede from the rest of the state or that Rector would attempt to bypass the assembly by taking the issue directly to the state legislature, the Unionists agreed to a referendum to be held on the first Monday of August in which Arkansans would vote either "for secession" or "for cooperation."[43]

Despite the heated words and animosities that characterized the March convention, many Unionists and secessionists were largely in agreement on one major issue: any attempt to coerce the seceded states back into the Union would be legitimate grounds for the state to secede. Such an action, the delegates had declared, would be "resisted by Arkansas to the last extremity."[44] This was the Achilles heel of the Unionist position, and it put them at the mercy of events over which they had no control.[45]

For the time being, however, the state remained in the Union. In the northern and western portions of the state, many Arkansans were greatly relieved that the convention had refused to be stampeded into secession. Residents of Van Buren in Crawford County fired a thirty-nine-gun salute in honor of the thirty-nine delegates who had held firm against secession, and the town's two returning delegates were greeted by a cheering crowd and a brass band.[46]

But events hundreds of miles to the east would dramatically affect the course of affairs in the state. On April 11, after three months of negotiation and stalemate, Confederate authorities in South Carolina demanded the surrender of the federal garrison at Fort Sumter in Charleston Harbor. The demand was refused. At 4:30 a.m. on the following morning, April 12, 1861, Confederate gunners opened fire on Fort Sumter. The federal garrison surrendered the fort on April 14.

The following day, President Lincoln called for a force of 75,000 men to suppress the rebellion, including 780 men from Arkansas. Governor Rector's response came one week later. "In answer to your requisition for troops from Arkansas to subjugate the Southern States, I have to say that none will be furnished. The demand is only adding insult to injury. The people of this state are freemen, not slaves, and will defend to the last extremity, their honor, lives and property against Northern mendacity and usurpation."[47]

The attack on Fort Sumter and President Lincoln's subsequent call for troops dramatically altered the political situation in Arkansas. For secessionists, the attack was a political godsend, and even many who had staunchly clung to the Union now felt compelled to move into the secessionist camp. On April 20, John Brown, the Whig planter and Unionist from Camden who had strongly opposed secession, wrote in his diary, "The war feeling is aroused, the die is cast. The whole South will be aroused in two weeks."[48] *Gazette* editor Christopher Danley, another long-time opponent of secession, added, "Now that the overt act has been committed we should I think draw the sword, and not sheath it until we can have a guarantee of all of our rights, or such standards as will be honorable in the South."[49]

Governor Rector wasted no time in seizing the initiative. Though Arkansas had not formally left the Union, he ordered former senator Solon Borland to take command of the state militia and seize the federal outpost at Fort Smith, which they did without opposition. In late April, chairman David Walker reluctantly called for the state convention to reassemble at Little Rock on May 6 to once again consider the question of secession. Walker, a staunch Unionist, had been under extreme pressure since the attack on Sumter, and he was now convinced that Missouri and the other border states would soon secede. The convention assembled at ten in the morning before packed galleries. A motion was quickly made to prepare an ordinance of secession. The document was ready by 3:00 p.m., and the delegates reassembled to vote. The outcome was a foregone conclusion. A last desperate attempt by a few die-hard Unionists to submit the question to the people was overwhelmingly defeated, and the roll call proceeded in the tense and hushed chamber.[50]

In stark contrast to the vote of two months earlier, only five of the seventy delegates voted to remain in the Union. In response to the chairman's appeal for a unanimous vote, four of these added their names to the ordinance of secession. Only Isaac Murphy of Madison County refused to join the secessionists' bandwagon, noting that he could not "aid in bringing about the untold evils that would assuredly follow in the train of secession."[51] As he concluded his remarks, Mrs. Frederick Trapnall, the widow of a prominent Little Rock attorney and one of the leaders of the capital city's society, tossed a bouquet of flowers at Murphy's feet, but most in the packed galleries jeered in derision. Murphy's principled stand made little difference in the outcome. Shortly after 4:00 in the afternoon on May 6, 1861, Arkansas declared that it had severed its bonds with the Union, which it had so eagerly joined only twenty-five years earlier. The state now faced the greatest crisis in its history.[52]

The secession convention remained in session until June 3 to deal with other matters, but the near unanimity that had characterized the secession vote soon disappeared. The old-line Whigs and conservative elements in the Democratic Party were determined to ensure that radical secessionist elements did not take control of the convention. *Gazette* editor Danley had written to a friend, "I think the conservative men of the convention should take charge of the affairs of the state and prevent the wild secessionists from taking us to the Devil."[53] Notably, the five-man Arkansas delegation to the Confederate Congress was headed by Robert Ward Johnson, but the other four men had been Unionists before Sumter. The convention pointedly rejected Hindman's attempt to join the Confederate congress. "The Whig-Dynasty leaders simply did not want change to get out of hand, so they took control of the new government," James Woods has noted. "Thus the revolution against the Union would not become a revolution at home."[54]

A serious challenge to state unity soon arose in the mountainous regions in the north-central part of the state, where opposition to secession remained strong. By late 1861, a group of area residents formed a clandestine organization called the Arkansas Peace

Society, quite possibly the first organized resistance to a Confederate government anywhere in the seceded states. The first evidence of the society's existence appeared in Searcy and Izard counties in November of 1861. Pro-Confederate citizens in the two counties quickly arrested about fifty men suspected of membership in the organization, and, through promises of leniency and threats of violence, exacted the names of other members. The number of alleged members and the extent of the group's organization stunned Confederate authorities. The society had a constitution and a series of secret signs and passwords. A yellow ribbon attached to a cabin or a fencepost meant that a member resided there. If a member howled like a wolf, a fellow member would countersign by hooting like an owl. The greeting "It's a dark night," was to be answered with, "Not so dark as it will be before morning."[55]

By early December, the Searcy County militia had arrested dozens of suspected members of the society. Acting under orders from Governor Rector, the militia commander chained seventy-eight of them together in pairs and marched them under heavy guard to Little Rock, over ninety miles away. They were soon joined by detainees from Carroll, Van Buren, Marion, and Fulton counties. Izard County authorities adopted a different approach. Rather than face prison or worse in Little Rock, the accused men were given the "opportunity" of enlisting in the Confederate army. All accepted.[56]

This novel solution was soon adopted by Confederate authorities in Little Rock as well. The 117 alleged subversives who had been dispatched to the capital were given the option of standing trial for treason or joining the Rebel army. All but fifteen chose the latter. They were formed into two companies and shipped east of the Mississippi, where they saw action at Shiloh and other battles. The companies' reputations preceded them, and Confederate commanders, naturally, had little faith in the new recruits. In later years, one of the "volunteers" recalled the instructions of a Rebel officer to his

While the Unionists of the Arkansas Peace Society did not suffer from such violence as was portrayed in Thrilling Adventures of Daniel Ellis *in eastern Tennessee, many were imprisoned or forcibly enlisted in the Confederate army. Courtesy of Bill and Amy Gatewood.*

men just prior to the battle of Shiloh. "Boys, we are going to have a hell of a fight, and I have no confidence in these men sent here from Arkansas. If they try to get to the Federals, shoot them; if they fall back, shoot them; if they try to run, shoot them."[57]

Many did desert at the first opportunity, sometimes individually, other times in groups. After brief visits with their families, many of these made their way to Missouri where they enlisted in Federal service, comprising units that came to be known as "mountain Feds." Ironically, a grand jury failed to indict the fifteen men who had refused to enlist.[58]

The exact size of the Arkansas Peace Society remains a mystery, as do its goals and the motives of its members. Perhaps understandably, many of the arrested men contended that they had been misled or were unaware of what they were joining. One claimed that he had heard an oath read to him, but did not fully understand it because he was deaf. Still another contended that he was trapped into membership when he was asked whether he liked the old constitution or the new and answered that he knew nothing of either. One said that he would have joined the Confederate army if he had not been arrested. Another claimed that he had joined the Confederate army already, TWICE, and was ready to join again.[59]

But a member of the citizens' committee from Izard County wasn't buying any of this. He noted that they cheered when they heard the news (erroneous as it turned out) that the Confederates had been defeated at the Battle of Oak Hills (Wilson's Creek), and, "When I and several other gentlemen raised the *stars and bars* here, these very men threatened to come and pull them down.... [T]hey swore that they would never muster under the d____d nigger flag, but if any one would just come along with the stars and stripes that they would arise at midnight and go to it, and they would fight for it too when they got there." In a letter to Confederate president Jefferson Davis, Governor Rector wrote that there were 1,700 members of the organization in the state, although the names of only 240 are known.[60]

Historian Ted Worley has demonstrated that in the six counties involved, the ratio of slave to white population and the per capita wealth were significantly lower than in the state as a whole. Worley also concluded that the society's principal aim may have been just what it claimed, namely the protection of its members against all outside intruders, including robbers, runaway slaves, and Confederate authorities. "The society intended to protect itself at home," he writes, "not by rushing off to the Stars and Stripes. Left to itself in peaceful dissent, the brotherhood probably would have been merely a Unionist island of passive resistance. Drastic suppression by neighbors, acting in the name of the Confederacy, and harsh treatment by the military gave the members a fighting cause."[61] Northern and western Arkansas would continue to be Unionist strongholds throughout the course of the war. Despite having the third-smallest white population, Arkansas would provide more troops for the Federal Army than any other Confederate state except Tennessee.[62]

Obviously then, the crushing of the Peace Society did not put an end to secessionist sentiment in the state. By late 1862, signs of discontent were appearing in other parts of the state. In a recent study, historian Carl Moneyhon has demonstrated that resistance to Confederate authority in late 1862 and 1863 was strongest in southwest Arkansas, especially in the region south and west of the Saline River. Unlike the mountainous northwest, the southwestern part of the state had developing plantation agriculture and a significant slave population. Most of the counties in the region had given majorities to the pro-slavery candidate John C. Breckinridge in the presidential election of 1860 and had supported secession in both state conventions in 1861. After secession the region's young men rushed to enlist in the Confederate cause. Camden alone supplied thirteen companies (1,300 men or about three-fourths of the town's adult white male population in 1860) by September 1861, and 1,500 Union County men had enlisted in Confederate service.[63]

By the war's second winter, however, the early enthusiasm had given way to a widespread disenchantment. Theophilus Holmes, Confederate commander of the Department of the Trans-Mississippi, had taken note of this, writing in a December 1862 letter to Confederate president Jefferson Davis of "the growing disaffection to the war among the people." He attributed this disaffection to a variety of factors, including a food shortage brought on by a drought the previous summer, spiraling inflation, the failure to pay or adequately provision the soldiers, and discontent with the Confederacy's conscription laws, particularly the provision that exempted one white man on each plantation for every twenty slaves on the plantation. He informed the president that he could not control the situation without imposing martial law.[64]

In Camden, John Brown also noted a "good deal of excitement" in opposition to conscription, "especially on account of the exemption law, which exempts slave holders having twenty slaves." He went on to note that "some are still opposed to the war in toto. Some are unwilling to leave their families unprovided as they are[,] some have been in the army and have been dissatisfied with their treatment and the conduct of their officers." All of these factors had combined, he wrote, to create "a sprinkle of disloyalty beyond what was expected."[65]

In late January 1863, President Davis agreed to suspend the writ of *habeas corpus*, and Holmes declared martial law on February 9. He further authorized the raising of local units of partisan rangers to round up deserters and enforce the conscription laws and sent some regular army units to assist in the task.[66]

Resistance to Confederate authority took many forms, however, and proved difficult to suppress. In January, between forty and fifty draftees walked out of a conscript camp in Magnolia. February brought rumors of the formation of a secret organization dedicated to resisting conscription and advocating an end to the war and a return to the Union. Union Leagues sprang up in Calhoun, Clark, and Pike counties.[67]

That same month, a force of 250 mounted Confederates set out after a band of eighty-three Unionists and deserters led by an Arkadelphia Unionist named Andy Brown. Brown's band had committed a series of thefts in the Ouachita Mountains northwest of Arkadelphia. On February 15, the Confederates caught up with Brown near McGrew's Mill on the Walnut Fork of the Ouachita River, about halfway between Hot Springs and Mt. Ida. In the battle that ensued, the Confederates inflicted thirty-five casualties, took twenty prisoners, and captured a substantial quantity of provisions and stolen items, while suffering only one man killed and five wounded. About thirty of Brown's party fled north and crossed the swollen Ouachita River. The Confederates chose not to pursue them. Three weeks after the engagement at McGrew's Mill, Brown and twenty-seven survivors reported to Col. M. LaRue Harrison at Fayetteville, where some of them joined the First Arkansas Infantry Union.[68]

In Pike County, another band of dissidents launched attacks on area settlements from its base at a mountain pass near the head of the Little Missouri River. A group of area residents attacked the band's stronghold, killing some outright and capturing and hanging two of the ringleaders. Calhoun County authorities rounded up and hanged three members of the local Union League. Confederate military courts were also set up to prosecute disloyal elements. Since no records were kept of these proceedings, the extent of the actions taken by these courts is impossible to assess, though some Unionists later insisted that hundreds of deserters were tried and executed by the courts.[69]

Despite these harsh actions, dissent and resistance to authority persisted. Confederate agents sent to the region in the fall of 1863 reported that anti-Confederate sentiment had actually increased. One noted that in Columbia County there was "undoubtedly a Union sentiment prevailing among a large class of citizens here." More draconian measures followed. John Brown noted, "The military have been sent out to bring them [the dissidents] in and in some cases, some have [been] arrested & been shot or hung & others have left the country to join the enemy." A Union officer returning from the region in 1864 reported, "Every conceivable means has been used to force [these men] into the rebel service; they have been hung by scores; they have been hunted down with blood hounds by the slaveholding rebels of the Red river Valley; they have been robbed of their property, chained and imprisoned." Still the resistance continued.[70]

One area newspaper described the disloyal elements as "deserters, disaffected persons, and turbulent characters," and Confederate authorities often portrayed them as little more than jayhawkers and bandits. Some undoubtedly were, but the available evidence clearly indicates that much of the opposition was class-based. At Camden, John Brown recorded in his diary that many of the resisters were "poor men whose families are unprovided at home," and Clark County editor Samuel M. Scott wrote to Governor Flanagin that "the cry of poor men being obliged to fight for the rich may be heard on all sides."[71]

Carl Moneyhon has concluded that "from the beginning those who fought for the Confederacy came to see themselves as poor men who were having to fight a war to benefit rich men. Their own opportunities were being squandered in a conflict that had no goal other than the protection of slavery. Their fight was not only with conscription but also with the ruling class."[72] This internal dissent ate away at the state's morale and caused Confederate authorities to detach badly needed troops to deal with the situation. The extent to which this discontent manifested a growing Unionist sentiment in the state is open to debate. But it is clear that something more than brigands and outlaws were involved in the resistance to Confederate authority. And the fact that many of the dissidents ended up wearing Union blue is a fact that cannot be ignored or dismissed.

Of course, nothing provided an incentive for the demonstration of loyalty to the Union like the presence of Federal soldiers. After Pine Bluff was occupied by Federal cavalry in October 1863, many Pine Bluff citizens voluntarily took an oath of loyalty to the Union, causing one surprised citizen of the town to remark, "There are more union people here and in L[itttle]. R[ock]. than anyone ever thought."[73]

As prospects of a Confederate victory dimmed and hardships on civilians multiplied, disillusionment with the war increased. In a letter to "My Old Friend Gov. H. Flanagin," probably written in late 1863, Maurice Smith, a prominent Tulip (Dallas County) slaveowner, confessed that he had been "carried away with the multitude under the pressure and excitement" of the secession crisis. "Since that time, serious and sober reflection" had led him to believe "that we were too hasty in the matter." Over the course of the past few months, the "strength and position of the enemy" combined with "the disaffection with the soldiery and the gloomy prospect for subsistence on our part, the distress and disaffection throughout the length and breadth of our state," had convinced Smith "that the people would tomorrow, if not restrained, vote the state back into the Union by an overwhelming majority. Secession is dead—the principle was wrong, although advocated by us both." He added that significant numbers of other Arkansans, "many of them men of prominence" had also "tamed down on that question. You would be astonished could I name them."[74]

Smith assured Flanagin that "I am not a traitor to the South, by no means; but when I contemplate the suffering and horrors of this war already in our state, my heart shudders, and to picture in my mind its continuance, the very thought sickens me." He closed with an appeal to the governor: "It would be the noblest act of your life to step forward and acknowledge the great error of secession, and to give the people the power to reconsider and act for themselves in this matter." Smith never mailed his letter, but the sentiments he expressed provide clear evidence that disaffection with the war and desire for a return to the Union were widespread and transcended class lines.[75]

So what are we to make of this significant spirit of Unionism in what was, at least nominally, a Confederate state? What if the

Unionists had prevailed in 1861 and Arkansas had remained in the Union? These are matters about which we can only speculate. But it is clear that Unionism in Arkansas was not confined to a few counties in northern and northwestern Arkansas. Rather it was powerful and widespread force from the beginning of the war until the end, and one that powerfully influenced the course of events in the state in that tragic period from 1861 to 1865.

"When the Arks. boys goes by they take the rags off the bush": Arkansans in the Wilson's Creek Campaign of 1861

William Garrett Piston
Missouri State University

On July 23, 1861, John Johnson—a forty-seven-year-old Pulaski County resident and soldier in the First Arkansas Mounted Riflemen—penned a letter while sitting in his unit's camp near the Missouri border. He was fully confident in himself and his fellow soldiers who had so recently enlisted in Confederate service. With scant attention to grammar or punctuation, Johnson wrote: "Dear Mother I am in high hopes that we may all succeed in getting home safe and with glory and liberty overflowing in our hearts to see the pleasures that we have seen to gether and if not in this world I hope and pray to God that we shall meet in a better world above and I expect to try to do right as well as I know how."[1] Five days later, having entered Missouri, Johnson wrote to his wife, Lucy: "The boys are burning for a battle. If you could see them when the news comes in a working on their arms. They shine like new money and when on parade they are all as regular as clock pendlams.... when the Arks. boys goes by they take the rags off the bush."[2]

John Johnson was killed at the Battle of Wilson's Creek on August 10, 1861. His eldest son, Pleasant Johnson, also died there. A second son, Harrison, survived the battle but was killed the following year. Lucy Johnson, age forty-eight, was left to care for two remaining sons and two daughters. The Johnsons were yeomen farmers. Their family's tragedy was not unusual for thousands of

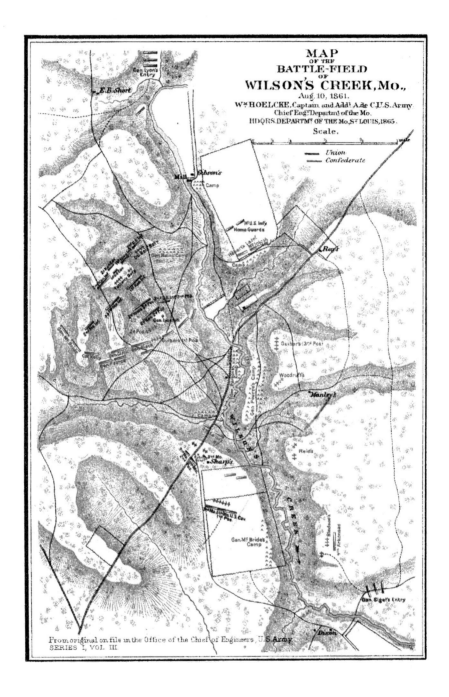

white Arkansans who decided to support the Confederacy. It did, however, occur early, at a time when it was still possible to believe in a short conflict, one that would bring honor to its participants. "I am well satisfied with soldiering," Johnson had written in an earlier letter. "We can whip five to one."[3]

Almost 3,500 Arkansas troops took part in the Wilson's Creek campaign, May–August 1861, which culminated on August 10 in the second major Confederate victory of the war. An unknown number of slaves accompanied them, as did a few white women who were wives of officers. Almost no information has survived concerning the white women who chose to share their menfolks' ordeal, and even less about the enslaved African Americans who were forced to accompany their masters. The role and experiences of the soldiers themselves, however, can be traced in some detail, and not just in terms of strategy and tactics. Thanks to the manner in which troops were raised, and because neither the Confederacy nor the Arkansas state government was initially prepared to support the large numbers who flocked to the flag, the war in 1861 was very much a community experience. No one was unaffected by the conflict, and the relationship between soldiers and their hometowns is an important part of the story.

The Arkansans in the Wilson's Creek campaign served in either the Confederate army[4] or the Arkansas State Troops, an organizational awkwardness that reflected circumstances peculiar to the state. Prior to the conflict, two types of militia served in Arkansas. There was the county-based militia guaranteed under the Second Amendment to the U.S. Constitution and organized under Arkansas state law. But this was supplemented by volunteer militia companies, which were also subject to state law. While both had fallen somewhat into abeyance with the removal of any serious Indian threat, both enjoyed a revival in 1860, as sectional tensions increased. Pulaski County, for example, had four militia units in

1860: the "Capital Guards," the "Peyton Rifles," the "Totten Artillery," and the "Pulaski Light Cavalry."[5] Like other Arkansans, these soldiers became enmeshed in the complex events by which their state left the Union.

When South Carolina seceded in December 1860, the Arkansas legislature called for a convention of delegates to consider the state's relationship to the national government. The convention met in February 1861, voted to take no immediate action, and adjourned. Early that same month, some 5,000 militiamen congregated in Little Rock, threatening to seize the federal arsenal there. Governor Henry M. Rector, who strongly favored secession, proclaimed this to be a spontaneous gathering. His complicity remains a source of debate among historians. In any case, Rector convinced the U.S. Army captain commanding the arsenal's sixty-five-man garrison to avoid bloodshed by withdrawing to St. Louis. Then on February 22, the seven states of the Deep South that had left the Union organized the Confederate States of America. Sentiment in Arkansas remained sharply divided until April, when the Confederates fired upon Fort Sumter in Charleston, South Carolina, and President Abraham Lincoln called for 75,000 militia to suppress what he considered to be a domestic rebellion. The Arkansas convention was called back into secession, but before it met, Governor Rector directed the state militia to capture Fort Smith, located on the Arkansas River in the northwestern portion of the state. Since the federal garrison had fled, the post fell without a shot being fired. On May 6, the state convention voted to take Arkansas out of the Union; the state joined the Confederacy on May 18.[6]

Governor Rector and the state convention were soon at odds, as the convention remained in session, in part because the state legislature was adjourned and not scheduled to meet for some time. As a challenge to the governor's power, and to provide for the immediate defense of the state, the convention on May 30 created a

Military Board and called for volunteers to join a new militia organization, which was sometimes labeled the "Army of Arkansas," but more often simply the "Arkansas State Troops." Thus during the spring and summer, three distinct organizations competed for recruits across the state: the Confederate army, the Arkansas militia, and the Arkansas State Troops. Significant confusion ensued when units in the different organizations received identical numerals, or when units in one force transferred to another. The "Totten Light Battery," for example, began as a state militia unit in Pulaski County in 1860 but joined the Arkansas State Troops en masse in May 1861.[7]

Regardless of their type of unit, the Arkansans who served in the Wilson's Creek campaign entered the service in a similar manner, sharing cultural experiences that reflected the importance of community in their lives. Although the issues were national, they were experienced and worked out at the local level. This was an era when party loyalties were strong, and, with no secret ballot, people knew how their neighbors voted. Lincoln's call in April for volunteers to coerce the South fostered spontaneous mass meetings at the town or county level across the state. While resolutions criticized the central government and defended the rights of the states, no one doubted the primary cause of the war. For example, Calhoun County citizens adopted a resolution condemning the Republican Party for "having at heart the annihilation of slavery, our dearest and most endeared institution," while the citizens of Johnson County paraded to salute the flag of the Confederacy as "the white man's flag."[8]

When Arkansas left the Union in May, another round of community meetings followed, as men flocked to join to the colors. Men, women, and children met in town halls, churches, general stores, or any available structure. There were endless patriotic speeches and often public prayers. Following instructions from

Governor Rector and the Military Board, the citizens organized companies that would proceed to designate rendezvous points, where they would be combined into numbered regiments. The company, which usually numbered eighty to one hundred men, was thus the primary level of organization. Companies were almost always drawn from a single town or county, which meant that the volunteers knew each other. The men usually elected both their officers and noncommissioned officers. Competition could be fierce, and the men who won out were often those who had furnished considerable sums of money to equip the unit. Donations of whiskey were not unknown either.

Despite occasional bribery, however, the soldiers took the elections seriously. The highest ranks almost always went to prominent and respected men of the community, sometimes men who had fought in the Mexican War or had some other military experience. For example, thirty-four-year-old Harris Flanagin, who organized a company for Confederate service from Pulaski County, was a Northerner by birth. After teaching school, he studied law and moved to Arkansas in 1839. He served in a militia company during the Mexican War and was elected to both the state Senate and House of Representatives.[9] Dandridge McRae, age thirty-two, came from a prominent slaveholding family in Alabama. A graduate of South Carolina College, he arrived in Searcy, Arkansas, in 1849, where he practiced law and was grandmaster of the local Masonic lodge. He began raising a Confederate regiment, but was soon sidetracked by being appointed inspector general for the Arkansas State Troops.[10] Thomas J. Churchill, an officer in a regiment of mounted infantry during the Mexican War, organized a similar unit in 1861. The thirty-seven-year-old Little Rock postmaster was a native of Kentucky who settled in Arkansas in 1848. After marrying into a wealthy slaveholding family, he established his own plantation, named "Blenheim" in honor of the Duke of Marlborough's famous 1704 victory.[11] William Edward Woodruff Jr., age thirty, was the son of the state's leading newspaper editor. Born to wealth and privilege, he graduated from the Western Military Institute but practiced law. He captained the "Totten Battery" in 1861. Forty-one-year-old Benjamin T. Embry, who recruited a company at Galla Rock, could not match Flanagin, McRae, Churchill, or Woodruff in wealth or social prominence, yet he was a prosperous farmer and the leading merchant in his own community.[12]

Raised independently, these early war companies usually adopted names that reflected their connection with their county or hometown: "Des Arc Rangers" (Des Arc); "Chicot Rangers" (Chicot County); "Johnson Rifles" (Johnson County); "Lawrence Rifles" (Lawrence County); "Pulaski Rangers" (Pulaski County); "Yell Rifles" (Yell County); "Independence Rifles" (Independence County)—to give but a few examples.[13] Because neither the Confederate nor the Arkansas state government was immediately prepared to equip the rush of volunteers, those who went to war in the spring of 1861 initially relied on their home communities for almost everything except their firearms and accoutrements. Uniforms, shoes, haversacks, canteens, mess equipment, blankets, tents, and other such items were all supplied locally. Women played an especially important role in this community-wide effort, in part through their skills as seamstresses, and hometown papers were quick to recognize them. In Little Rock, where several companies were raised simultaneously, the *Arkansas True Democrat* was effusive with praise. "The ladies of Little Rock have worked day and night for months making uniforms," noted an article printed in mid-summer. The women spent their own money and "neither charged nor received one cent of remuneration for any service."[14]

A complex reciprocal relationship developed between hometowns and "their" volunteers. The town helped to equip the soldiers and raised large sums of money to support the families of the soldiers during their absence. The town also pledged to care for widows and orphans. In return, the soldiers pledged that their conduct in camp and battle would uphold the honor of their hometowns. This implicit social contract reveals Arkansans' strong sense of corporate honor. The soldiers carried their community's reputation into the field with them, and were expected to give an accounting upon their return.[15] Almost every company went off to war with a concrete symbol of corporate honor, in the form of a flag sewn by the ladies of their hometown. Such flags were presented in public ceremonies, where the relationship between the soldiers and the community was explicitly articulated. Like many units, the "Hempstead Cavalry" received a flag just before leaving for its rendezvous point. In her dedication speech, Miss Belle Smith announced: "On behalf of the ladies of Bois D'Arc Township, I have the honor to present you with this military ensign. It is the workmanship of the daughters of the South; it is baptized with the warm affection of gushing hearts, and consecrated by their prayers."[16] Women expressed expectations of "their" soldiers clearly, even while employing the florid oratory of the day. In Carroll County, Josephine Wright and a Miss Baily sewed a banner for the local company. When presenting it, Miss Wright proclaimed to the assembled soldiers:

> Should the proud bird of liberty 'ere cease to nestle amid our hills ... or cease to flap triumphantly its broad wings o'er our lovely valleys, smiling in perpetual beauty? 'Twill be after the graceful folds of this beautiful banner have mingled in the dust. I feel assured that when it waves no longer in proud defiance, the last of this gallant number shall have fallen, nobly fallen, on the "bosom of our Sunny South."[17]

In other words, Miss Wright expected the Carroll County soldiers to die to the last man rather than disgrace the banner, and by implication, their home community. When Mattie Faulkner presented a flag to Thomas Churchill's men, she clearly expected the banner to serve as a concrete reminder to the soldiers of their duty, and of the continued support of the folks back home. She declared:

> That you may be ever reminded of these objects of your reverence and affection, and of their gratitude and admiration, their unceasing prayers and benedictions, we have made you this banner, and it is with pride and pleasure that I now commit it, on their behalf, to your faithful keeping. Let it be borne aloft into the thickest of the fight—up to the highest eminence of honor. Let the sight of it animate and encourage you, nerving you in the hour of trial to the utmost pitch of fortitude and courage![18]

With flags flying and the well-wishes of loved ones ringing in their ears, individual companies of Arkansans moved to various rendezvous points. Those who arrived at Little Rock or Fort Smith came into contact with the two men who would command them at the Battle of Wilson's Creek: Ben McCulloch and Nicholas Bartlett Pearce. McCulloch was a hero of the Mexican War and a former Texas Ranger. Newly commissioned a brigadier in the Confederate service, he was responsible for the defense of the Indian Territory. For logistical reasons, he made his headquarters at Fort Smith on the Arkansas River. The Confederate government eventually named Brigadier General William J. Hardee the top Confederate commander for Arkansas, but he did not arrive until the Wilson's Creek campaign was well under way. Thus, by default, the defense of northern Arkansas became McCulloch's concern. The self-taught McCulloch despised West Pointers, which was unfortunate, as circumstances forced him to work closely with "Bart" Pearce, who graduated from the military academy in 1850. Thirty-four years old and a native of Kentucky, Pearce resigned his commission in 1858 and joined his father-in-law's mercantile business in Osage Mills, Arkansas. Like many in his adopted state, Pearce opposed leaving the Union but believed that Lincoln's decision to coerce the seceded states left Arkansans no choice but to join the Confederacy. The Military Board appointed Pearce a brigadier general commanding the First or Western Division of the Army of Arkansas.[19] As such, his recruitment of men for the Arkansas State Troops was in direct competition with McCulloch. It appears, however, that men joined either the Confederate service or the Arkansas State Troops more or less at random, without giving much thought to the distinctions between the two. Almost everyone expected the war to be over before cold weather set in.

As companies arrived at Little Rock, Fort Smith, and various designated camps, McCulloch and Pearce began forming them into regiments. McCulloch's Confederate brigade included a Louisiana infantry unit and a regiment of cavalry from Texas, but the bulk of its men were Arkansans. Colonel Thomas J. Churchill led the First Arkansas Mounted Riflemen. Colonel James McQueen McIntosh, commanding the Second Arkansas Mounted Riflemen, held his position more or less by accident. A Florida native and a West Pointer, he had been stationed at Fort Smith and resigned his commission just prior to the post's capture by the Arkansas militia. Colonel Dandridge McRae was still recruiting his Confederate infantry regiment. His men participated in the Wilson's Creek campaign without receiving a numerical designation; they were usually labeled "McRae's Battalion, Arkansas Volunteers." Pearce's Arkansas State Troops included five infantry regiments. Those destined to fight at Wilson's Creek were the Third Infantry (Colonel John Rene Gratiot); the Fourth Infantry (Colonel Jonathan D. Walker); and the Fifth Infantry (Colonel Thomas Pleasant Dockery). Pearce had two artillery units, each with four guns: the "Fort Smith Light Battery," commanded by Captain John G. Reid, and the Totten Light Battery (soon renamed the "Pulaski Light Battery"), commanded by Captain William Woodruff. Captain

Sgt. Tom Spence of the Second Arkansas Mounted Rifles was among the Arkansawyers who saw their first combat in the bitter fighting at Wilson's Creek. Courtesy of the Old State House Museum.

Charles A. Carroll led a small undesignated cavalry company, usually called "Carroll's Cavalry," while Captain Americus V. Reiff led a small unit of horsemen, "Reiff's Arkansas Cavalry Company." Pearce eventually loaned Reiff and his men to McCulloch, who employed them as his bodyguard and as scouts. Pearce used Carroll's horsemen as his own bodyguard. In addition, there was a large unit of horsemen commanded by Colonel DeRosey Carroll, usually labeled "First Cavalry."[20]

While McCulloch and Pearce considered the larger strategic issues, the men under them stayed in touch with their homes as best they could by mail. Their letters included anxious inquiries about family and friends, as well as the circumstances of their farms or businesses. They also discussed their adjustment to military life and related news about the men in their units, knowing that the information would be quickly disseminated throughout their communities. "I think I will make a tolorable good soldier," wrote Private Ras Stirman to his sister. "We have just finished our breakfast & the boys are

Dandridge McRae proudly described the battalion he led at Wilson's Creek as "six hundred men, the wildest blood in the South. They are however the best men in the whole state." Courtesy of Anthony Rushing.

washing the dises. Tell Aunt Emma that her boys are all well. Clay and Dick Powell are a little sick but will be up in a day or two."[21] John Johnson, who had been elected a lieutenant, informed his wife, "We are all well at this time and getting along tolerably well." He assured her that "the boys from our settlement is all well only Wm. Ellis Hayden is unwell." After some complaints about the poor quality of his rations, he concluded, "We hear a goodell of talk of fighting and we are preparing for a tight conflict."[22]

But how well prepared would the Arkansans be? The officers and men were certainly confident. "The Desha county cavalry is as fine a body of soldiers as it has been my fortune to see—each man looks every inch a soldier," wrote one correspondent to a Little Rock newspaper. He further claimed that the "Jackson guards would make the eyes of Frederick the Great glisten." From Van Buren, near Fort Smith, another correspondent wrote: "The troops are in most excellent health—have been very well drilled."[23] Such comments were meant for public consumption, of course, but Dandridge McRae was even more effusive about his men in his private correspondence to his wife. He wrote: "I am here in command of some six hundred men, the wildest blood in the South. They are however the best men in the whole state. It makes the heart of any true friend of Arkansas thrill with pride to see what men we are enabled to turn out. There is no drunkenness, no noise, no confusion, and they cheerfully turn out to obey every order."[24]

McRae's objectivity toward his own men may be questioned, of course. But he also made (or oversaw) a series of inspections that revealed great diversity among the Arkansas soldiers in terms of preparedness. Levels of training and discipline varied widely, with few units receiving high marks. McRae observed only one company armed exclusively with hunting weapons brought from home. But many were deficient in the number and types of arms they possessed, and there was much discontent over the manner in which arms captured from the federal arsenal at Little Rock were distributed. Most units apparently possessed antiquated smoothbore percussion or flintlock muskets. Clothing and shoes were an even greater problem. McRae's reports on individual units contained such remarks as:

> **Clothing:** Almost none, many of the men ragged and bare-footed.
> **Military Appearance:** Bad owing to want of almost everything.
> **Clothing:** Bad. Some of the men barefooted.
> **Clothing:** Very poor, some barefooted and nearly neked.[25]

On the other hand, Captain W. C. Corcovan's company stands as an example of what constituted for the times a particularly well-equipped unit. The company possessed twenty percussion and sixty-one flintlock muskets, together with cartridge boxes, waist belts, bayonets, and canteens. Corcovan spent $150 (apparently his own money) to purchase twenty-eight blankets, thirty-four pairs of shoes, thirty hats, fifty shirts, twenty pairs of underwear, one hundred fifty pairs of pants and blouses, and sixty tin cups and plates. The company also owned some cooking equipment and at least one tent.[26]

It is uncertain whether the pants and blouses Corcovan obtained were uniforms or civilian clothing, but the Arkansans serving under McCulloch and Pearce wore a mixture of both, with civilian clothing predominating. A small number of units wore fancy prewar militia uniforms. Others wore uniforms hastily sewn by the loved ones in their home towns. Blue and gray were equally popular colors, neither having any significance early in the war. The "Pulaski Light Battery" wore gray jeans uniforms with wide red trim, while one infantry company, the "Pike Guards," wore "full dress suits of green with buff trim."[27] It was also common for soldiers to wear civilian clothing adorned with colorful trim to achieve something like a military appearance. Most, however, simply wore what Pearce described as "citizen's clothing."[28]

While historians have yet to make a detailed sociological study of the Arkansas volunteers of 1861, a cursory examination of muster rolls suggests that the company led by Captain C. L. Lawrence was typical. Lawrence was a native of Kentucky, a twenty-eight-year-old lawyer with no previous military experience. He commanded thirteen officers and eighty-three privates, all but eight of whom were born in the South. Four were Northerners, two were Germans, and two were Irish. The overwhelming majority were farmers, but the ranks included teachers, carpenters, and blacksmiths, together with a wood chopper, a painter, a distiller, and a ditcher. The youngest members of the company were William M. Sisco, age fifteen, and James H. Chateen, sixteen, both of whom stood only five feet tall. The oldest member was Maston K. White, forty-seven, a farmer originally from South Carolina.[29]

As the Arkansans adjusted to military life, circumstances in Missouri began to draw them closer toward conflict. In June, Brigadier General Nathaniel Lyon, commanding Federal forces in St. Louis, initiated a campaign to destroy the Missouri State Guard. Missouri had not passed an ordinance of secession, but Lyon knew that Governor Claiborne Fox Jackson favored secession. Lyon drove the state legislature from the capital, Jefferson City, in June. Three columns of Federals swept across the state, skirmishing with the State Guard and driving most of it into the Ozarks region in the southwestern corner of the state. The field commander of the State Guard, Major General Sterling Price, sought help from McCulloch. The Confederate commander feared that Lyon would invade Arkansas. He understood the advantage of a forward defense but was hesitant to enter Missouri. While considering what to do, he and Pearce began shifting some troops north to positions nearer the Missouri border.[30]

Many of the Arkansans were eager to help their Missouri neighbors who favored the Confederacy. They also possessed strong prejudices against German Americans, whom they mislabeled "Dutch." German Americans were known for their support of the Republican Party and abolitionism, and they made up a very large portion of the troops under Lyon's command. Ras Stirman, who had been promoted to sergeant, made a typical comment when he wrote his sister, "I would like to See you once more but it cant be So until after we whip the dutch."[31] In a similar fashion, John Johnson asked his wife to "tell old Uncle Lewis that Jas. is anctious to meet a Black Dutch."[32] The first chance, at least for some of the Arkansans, came in July. When a column of men under Colonel Franz Sigel, one of Lyon's subordinates, began moving west from Springfield, Missouri, toward camps of the Missouri State Guard near Carthage, Sterling Price asked McCulloch for assistance. The Confederate authorities in Richmond had already granted the Texan permission to enter Missouri should he deem it the best way to defend Arkansas, so on July 4 he rushed a column of horsemen across the state line. James McIntosh commanded the ad hoc brigade, which contained both Confederate units and Arkansas State Troops. Although they were too late to participate in the Missouri State Guard's victory over Sigel at Carthage on July 5, they did capture a 137-man detachment the Federals had stationed at Neosho. McIntosh returned to Arkansas with one hundred captured rifles and seven wagons filled with provisions.[33]

For the next three weeks the soldiers of Arkansas occupied camps near the Missouri line, often on scant rations thanks to a line of communications that ran across the rugged Boston Mountains back to the main supply base at Fort Smith. While the Arkansans drilled under the hot sun, Price assembled more than 7,000 men at Cowskin Prairie, in the extreme southwestern corner of Missouri. Lyon, however, concentrated more than 5,000 men in Springfield. Rather than wait for the Federals to move farther south, McCulloch agreed to join forces with Price for an attack on Springfield. The Arkansans moved north again, this time in a force about 5,000 strong. By July 31, McCulloch's Confederate brigade, Pearce's Arkansas State Troops, and Price's Missouri State Guard had come together near Cassville, Missouri. As the prospect of battle loomed, most of the Arkansans remained eager, but some failed to measure up to expectations. John J. Walker, a company commander in Pearce's brigade, confessed to a friend that two of his men had deserted. He continued:

> There is several others now in the company who stated publicly that they would go no further than the state line, and endeavored to induce others to join them. When we got to the line they halted for a moment, but the number that stopped with them being small they fell into the ranks again. I am in hopes there will be no more desertions from my Co., but there is no telling anything about white men in a campaign like this. Some of the very men who were most anxious for a fight when we left home, and men that I thought the best grit in the ranks, are among those wanting to get off.[34]

Price and Pearce agreed that McCulloch should command the combined Southern force, styled the Western Army. Writing long after McCulloch and Price were dead, Pearce claimed that he had taken the initiative, suggesting to Price that they both offer to serve under McCulloch's command. Price's adjutant, Thomas L. Snead, wrote a similar postwar story, implying that such deference was necessary in order to convince McCulloch to take the offensive. Both accounts err. The Arkansas Military Board had already placed Pearce and his men under McCulloch's command, and the Texan was enthusiastic about an offensive campaign. McCulloch's caution stemmed from a low opinion of Price's ability, the Missouri State Guard's minimal training, and the acute shortage of ammunition among the three forces.[35]

McCulloch directed the Western Army up the Wire or Telegraph Road, the main thoroughfare between Springfield and Fort Smith. Lyon anticipated his advance and moved toward the Southerners along the same route. Both sides acted with caution, however, and after some skirmishing on August 3 at Dug Springs, Lyon withdrew to Springfield. McCulloch's force advanced to within nine miles of the town, camping on August 6 along the valley of Wilson Creek (mislabeled Wilson's Creek by the soldiers). There, food from local farms and water from springs could sustain the Southern army while McCulloch scouted the Federal position in Springfield.[36]

Because of intense heat and a shortage of water, the march from Cassville to the camp at Wilson Creek was one of the most demanding of the war. "The last three days have indeed been hard days and nights," Dandridge McRae informed his wife. "We have had a hard time marching. What little sleep we had we lay down upon the naked ground without anything to be on or cover with. It is so hot and dusty that we can not bear the weight of a coat."[37] William Woodruff of the "Pulaski Battery" recalled, "It was fearfully hot and the men were on the verge of exhaustion." Fatigued infantrymen "swarmed about our guns on the road, hoping and begging for a ride." At the end of the march "the men fell where they halted, and went to sleep where they lay, supperless."[38]

The trek and brief skirmishing with the enemy also introduced many Arkansans to their first taste of the wider consequences of war. Lyon's army was critically short of rations and discipline in some of his regiments collapsed during their withdrawal to Springfield. The Federals looted civilian property indiscriminately, even though many of the locals were staunch Unionists. Dandridge McRae was shocked by what he observed. He informed his wife: "I am confirmed in my determination to die before an invading army shall pilfer my home. You dear wife can have no conception of the horrors of war—women violated, robbed of provisions, bed clothes, and all they have—and then left to starve."[39]

Between August 6 and August 9, McCulloch strove to obtain information about Lyon's dispositions in Springfield. The Arkansans enjoyed the rest, but tension mounted steadily as the prospect of an engagement grew ever more likely. Harris Flanagin was acutely aware that despite the toughening effects of the last few weeks, the Southerners would be going into battle with minimal training. But he took comfort in the fact that the enemy's men were equally raw. "I wish the troops were better drilled," he wrote, "but from what I can learn there has been no good fighting on either side in this section."[40]

For many, thoughts turned to their loved ones at home. "I would give anything to See you. I miss you So much," Ras Striman confessed to his sister. Realizing his helplessness amid larger events he confided, "Sis I shall enter the battle with a brave heart trusting on God for help. I have no fears when he is on our Side." The unusual juxtapositions of a soldier's life is underscored by the fact that the very next sentence following Stirman's poignant declaration of faith was a request that his sister send him some shirts.[41] The ever florid Dandridge McRae was very much concerned about his reputation. "I may never see you again," he informed his wife. "Though I shall never hear the patter of the little feet of my children, yet I leave to you and my children the heritage of an honorable name."[42] His preoccupation was not frivolous. In the male-dominated society of Victorian America, where most people still lived in small, close-knit communities, a man's reputation impacted his entire family. McRae and the other Arkansans facing battle were acutely aware that their behavior in the upcoming combat would reflect not only upon themselves, but also upon the honor of their extended kinfolk and their hometown.

Pressured by Price, McCulloch on August 9 ordered the army to assemble for a night march up the Wire Road, to attack Springfield at dawn. Events did not go as planned, however, for it began to rain. Pearce recalled that "as much of the ammunition was carried in canvas bags or haversacks, there was great danger that the powder and cartridges would be ruined in the rain."[43] McCulloch canceled the march but failed to repost the pickets that normally guarded the army against surprise. While the Southerners paused, Nathaniel Lyon acted. Undeterred by the weather, he split his men into two columns and marched out of Springfield during the early evening of August 9. At dawn on the August 10, a column under Lyon's direction struck the northern end of McCulloch's camp, while a second column under Franz Sigel attacked simultaneously from the south.[44]

Although McCulloch was caught by surprise, he responded to the crisis effectively, calling troops out of their camps and directing them to key points on the field. This meant, however, that each unit's camping spot determined its initial role in the battle. The Western Army's camp stretched along the valley of Wilson Creek, from a grist mill owned by John Gibson in the north to the broad fields of farmer Joseph Sharp in the south. The Arkansas infantry in McCulloch's Confederate brigade, McRae's Battalion, was camped on a slightly elevated plateau on the east side of the creek, near the Wire Road ford. McIntosh's Second Arkansas Mounted Riflemen were nearby. The majority of Pearce's Arkansas State Troops shared the plateau, with camps stretching southward almost to the Sharp farm. Perhaps because of his West Point training, Pearce had examined the surrounding terrain carefully with an eye to defense when the army first went into camp. He had placed Woodruff's "Pulaski Light Battery" to the north, on a ridge overlooking the Wire Road, and Reid's "Fort Smith Light Battery" to the south, near a junction of farm roads on a rise above Wilson Creek. He made his headquarters adjacent to Reid.[45]

Bart Pearce was the first high-ranking Southern commander to realize that the Western Army was under attack. A short while after dawn, a sergeant from Carroll's Cavalry rushed to his headquarters with alarming news. While drawing water from a spring east of the camps, he had been fired upon by Federal troops. Pearce called his men to arms and sent the sergeant to inform McCulloch. He ordered

Woodruff's artillerists to go into battery where they were, sending Gratiot's Third Infantry to their support. He moved Reid's battery slightly south to higher ground, with Dockery's Fifth Infantry positioned to assist them. He kept Walker's Fourth Infantry at his center, ready to respond to any threat. With these intelligent dispositions (soon approved by McCulloch), the commander of the Arkansas State Troops had protected the northern, southern, and eastern axes of his position on the plateau.[46] In reality there was no threat from the east. Pearce's sergeant had not encountered the main Federal force, but a small party detached from Sigel to guard the rear of his column during its circuitous march.

To the north, the "Pulaski Light Battery" was in action well before Pearce's orders arrived. Instead of attacking down the Wire Road, where his movement might be anticipated, Lyon's column traveled cross-country, moving over an unnamed broad hill, across Wilson Creek to the west of Woodruff's gunners. The hill would soon earn the nickname "Bloody Hill." Woodruff spotted Lyon's movement and opened fire. This helped to slow the Federal advance, giving Price more time to get the Missouri State Guard into position to face Lyon. McCulloch noted Woodruff's actions with approval and sent McRae's Battalion to support the battery. Not too long thereafter, the Third Infantry arrived to take up the same duty.[47] The infantrymen suffered moderately, but Woodruff's artillerymen had a hot time in the face of Federal counter-battery fire. "My boys stood it like heroes," Woodruff later wrote, adding that "not a man flinched, although the balls came like hail stones for all that time."[48]

A serious threat to Woodruff's position developed when a detachment of Federal infantry under Captain Joseph Plummer crossed Wilson Creek and advanced toward the battery, moving through the cornfields just north of it. The fields were part of a farm owned by John Ray. In response, Colonel James McIntosh led the Third Louisiana Infantry and his own Second Arkansas Mounted Riflemen (dismounted) up to the edge of the split-rail fence encircling Ray's corn, where they opened fire. After half an hour of close range combat, McIntosh led a charge that drove Plummer's men back across Wilson Creek. The Federals responded with artillery fire from "Bloody Hill," driving the Southerners back in a panic. The action in the Ray cornfield thus ended without a clear victor, but the Arkansans had helped to eliminate a serious threat to McCulloch's right flank.[49]

Back at the position of Reid's "Fort Smith Battery," Pearce waited for an attack from the east that never came. By turning his gaze to the southwest, however, he could see the Joseph Sharp farm, and he had witnessed something of the disaster that befell the Southern cavalry camped there when Sigel launched his attack, simultaneous to Lyon's movements on "Bloody Hill." After marching almost all night, Sigel reached a ridge overlooking the Sharp farm. At dawn, he opened a surprise artillery bombardment that scattered the 1,500 Southern cavalrymen camped at the farm. The fugitives included Churchill's First Arkansas Mounted Riflemen. Sigel then advanced into the Southern camps, breaking up their attempt to rally with another bombardment. Around 8:00 a.m., Sigel took up a position on the Wire Road, next to the Sharp farm house. He was directly in the rear of the Southern army, astride its line of communications.[50]

Pearce's inactivity during these developments is difficult to explain. In his official report and later writings, he cited the distance, confusion, and fear of hitting friendly troops as his reason for keeping his troops idle and his battery silent. Moreover, from his position across Wilson Creek, Pearce could see only a portion of the Sharp farm. Yet for a full thirty minutes after reaching the Wire Road, in plain sight of Pearce, Sigel's guns fired upon the rear of Price's Missourians as they fought on "Bloody Hill." If any question remained regarding the identity of Sigel's artillerymen, Pearce could have sent his bodyguard, "Carroll's Cavalry," to investigate.[51] Despite this negligence, Pearce did play a significant role in Sigel's defeat. While he waited, McCulloch acted, assembling a force of infantry (including part of McRae's Battalion) in low ground just in front of Sigel's position, an area hidden from Sigel's view that the Federal commander had failed to picket. When McCulloch launched a surprise attack on Sigel, Reid's "Fort Smith Battery" opened fire in support. Pearce stated that he opened fire when he saw Sigel's men wave a Stars and Stripes. The flag-waving incident did occur, just prior to McCulloch's charge. But Pearce also had a largely unobstructed view of McCulloch as he assembled his strike force, a mere 400 yards from the "Fort Smith Battery." Pearce's reference to the flag appears to have been an attempt to explain away his inactivity. In the elation of the Southern victory, no one called him to account. In any case, McCulloch's attack was wildly successful, driving Sigel's column off the field in disorder.[52]

While these events occurred, the First and Second Arkansas Mounted Riflemen joined the action on "Bloody Hill," where Price and the Missouri State Guard faced Lyon. After fighting dismounted in the Ray cornfield, the Second Rifles marched on foot across the ford of Wilson Creek. Since McCulloch had ordered McIntosh to assist him elsewhere, Lieutenant Colonel Benjamin T. Embry was in command. The Arkansans helped anchor the right flank of the Southern battle line. Their sister regiment, the First Rifles, rallied after being driven from the Sharp farm, and took up a position farther to the left. They also fought dismounted, with the exception of their commander, Churchill, who had one horse and then another shot from under him. The colonel's adjutant died at his side, "with his sword in hand, leading and cheering on the men." Two additional officers were killed and fourteen others wounded. This effectively gutted a critical level of the regiment's command structure, yet the non-commissioned officers carried on the fight quite effective-ly.[53] McRae's Battalion also took part, as the "Pulaski Battery" no longer needed protection. The terrain on "Bloody Hill" was open—mostly prairie grass with a scattering of oak trees. But the grass was waist high. Few men wore uniforms, and there was no standardiza-tion among those who did. There was no wind to stir regimental or company flags. "During the action it was impossible at any consid-erable distance to distinguish our friends from the enemy," McRae recalled.[54] Because the Southerners possessed on average only twen-ty-five rounds of ammunition per man, Price led the battle line slowly and cautiously up the hill, closing to well under one hundred yards before opening fire.

This Southern advance—the second of the day—failed. Although unknown to the Southerners, Lyon was killed during the combat. Major Samuel Sturgis took command of the Federals. As Price struggled to organize a third attack, he received substantial reinforcements from Pearce. The Arkansas commander first sent a section (two guns) from the "Fort Smith Battery" and seven com-panies of the Fifth Infantry across the creek. He soon followed, leading the Third Infantry in person. The "Pulaski Battery" shift-ed from its original position to one nearby and continued to fire upon the Federal positions on "Bloody Hill." It later crossed the creek to give even closer support.[55]

When the Southerners pushed up the hill a third time, Pearce led the combined Third and Fifth Arkansas as a miniature brigade, extending the Southern left flank. A fierce engagement lasting about thirty minutes ensued. Pearce and his fellow officers led from the front, winning high praise from their men, and casualties among the officers were heavy.[56] Writing twenty years after the bat-tle, Pearce recalled:

> The fortunes of the day were balanced in the scale, and some-thing must be done or the battle was lost. My men were eager to

go forward.... This proved to be the decisive engagement, and as volley after volley was poured against our lines, and our gallant boys were cut down like grass, those who survived seemed to be nerved to greater effort and a determination to win or die.[57]

Writing to his sister only a few hours after the battle ended, Private Ras Stirman of Gratiot's Third Infantry had a far less romantic view:

Sis it was a desperate affare. They march our regiment up a Slant right in the face of a battery and a large boddy of infantry. They were lying down in the brush and grass until we were within one hundred yards of them, then they opened up on us bringing us down like Sheep but we never waved. We did not wait for orders to fire but all of us cut loose at them like wild men, then we dropt to our nees and loded and Shot as fast as we could, we had to shoot by guess as they were upon the hill lying in the grass.[58]

Nor were the Federals the only danger. Gratiot reported: "During the action, I am sorry to say, we were very much annoyed [by] ... the fire of our own friends, who formed behind us and lower down upon the hill, and fired through my ranks after the fire had ceased from the enemy." Gratiot's unit took more than one hundred casualties, but he did not estimate what percentage came from friendly fire.[59]

Although the third Southern assault failed, a fourth one reached the top of "Bloody Hill," just as Sturgis withdrew the Federals in good order. Pearce joined McCulloch at the summit of the disputed ground, and there was a mutual understanding that the Southern army was too exhausted, and too short of ammunition, to consider a pursuit.[60]

After more than six hours of combat, the guns fell silent. The shock felt by the survivors, many of whom had never seen combat, must have been extreme. Harris Flanagin was deeply moved, writing:

But who can describe a battlefield? Over the ground at short intervals the dead and wounded are scattered. The wounded moaning and asking for water. Guns and weapons scattered everywhere. Here a dead horse, there a dead wagon or hospital carriage. I went through a portion of the field after the battle and found wounded men who could not speak make signs for water. I distributed what water I had and assisted in removing some of ours to the hospital.[61]

Care for the wounded now took priority. Since the Southerners had been caught by surprise, initial treatment of the wounded was haphazard. The Arkansas State Troops may have received better medical care than most. Pearce's brigade had an overall medical director, and each regiment seems to have had a surgeon.[62] The precise location of their aid stations is not known, but some of the physicians may have gone to John Ray's house, where a large field hospital was established. McCulloch had not appointed a medical director for his Confederate brigade, but casualties were treated by their regimental physicians. Dr. William A. Cantrell, attached to the First Arkansas Mounted Riflemen, described his experience vividly. "My work began soon after the first round or two of musketry," he wrote. "The wounded were then brought to me, and from that moment to the present time I have seen and heard nothing but gun-shot wounds and the groans of the dying and distressed. My Hospital was near the centre of the battleground."[63]

Although records are incomplete, at least ninety-one Arkansans lost their lives during the battle, and 303 were reported wounded. If one omits "Reiff's Arkansas Cavalry," "Carroll's Cavalry," and Walker's Fourth Infantry, which did not fire a shot, then 13.5 percent of the Arkansans engaged in combat became casualties. These losses were not distributed equally, however. Gratiot's Third Infantry lost 22 percent of its men, while Churchill's First Rifles lost 33 percent. An unknown number of men were simply missing. Among them was Captain William E. Gibbs, a Batesville, Arkansas, lawyer, who had raised a company for Churchill's regiment. A friend recalled: "Captain Gibbs was missing after the engagement. His bag, including company funds and the muster roll, was found in a tree along the waters of Wilson's Creek, and it was thought by some that he drowned though no body nor his horse were ever found."[64]

Captain Gibbs's comrades took it for granted that he had perished honorably, not deserted. The echo of gunfire had scarcely ended before the Arkansans who fought at Wilson's Creek began to think of their reputations. While this stemmed partly from ego, these citizen-soldiers we eager to prove that they had maintained the honor of their units, and by extension, the honor of their hometowns and loved ones. Flushed with success, the Arkansas regimental officers were effusive with praise in their battle reports, most of which were soon printed in papers across the state. Rank has its privileges, and officers got more credit than enlisted men. In a typical passage, Churchill wrote, "Too much praise cannot be bestowed upon the officers of my command, for they were ever seen in the thickest of the fight, cheering on their men, who always gallantly responded to the call."[65] McIntosh boasted, "My officers behaved in this first fight with great bravery and coolness."[66] Both Gratiot and Dockery congratulated all their officers and other ranks, but they also identified several companies by name as worthy of special praise, an indication of the degree to which company-level identities remained strong.[67]

Those Arkansans who had done little were sensitive about their contribution. DeRosey Carroll's First Cavalry spent all but a few minutes of the battle in reserve, making only a brief, unsuccessful charge against Federal battery on the far left flank of the line. Carroll noted, however, that his men, who had only eight rounds of ammunition apiece, discharged their weapons at very close range before retiring. "I am sure that our conduct will meet the approval of our country," he concluded.[68] Pearce was clearly aware that the reputation of troops in reserve might suffer. In his report, he went

out of his way to put their role in the best possible light. He laud-
ed the cavalry units of the Arkansas State Troops, although they
had done little but stand guard. He also had warm congratulations
for Lieutenant Colonel Frank Rector, who commanded the Fourth
Infantry due to Colonel Walker's illness. "I am particularly indebt-
ed to Colonel Rector for the ability [he] displayed during the
engagement," Pearce wrote. The men of the Fourth supported the
"Fort Smith Battery" all day and did not fire a shot. Yet Pearce
noted that Rector's men were "placed in a trying position, especially for new troops, grape shot, shell, and minie balls flying around
them and no chance of returning the fire."[69]

The reports written after Wilson's Creek were more than official documents dispatched to superiors. They were report cards to
the soldiers' home communities, appearing (as the writers intended) in hometown papers across Arkansas within less than two
weeks of the battle.[70] They also included long and very detailed lists
of the wounded, often giving specifics about a soldier's wound and
his prospects for recovery. There were no Purple Hearts for the
wounded, but word of their honorable sacrifices was widely and
speedily publicized, allowing their families and neighbors to bask
in their glory.[71]

Public and private scrutiny was acute because honor and reputation were on the line. Colonel Gratiot assured the editor of a
Washington County newspaper that the "Hempstead boys did their
work nobly, and fully sustained the good name of their city, and
were during the whole fight in the hottest fire."[72] J. M. Bailey, a soldier in the inactive Fourth Infantry, was particularly candid, writing: "How I envied the men of the commands that were engaged
and lost numbers in killed and wounded and felt humiliated that
my regiment fire not a shot nor shed one drop of blood!"[73] Harris
Flanagin confessed with apparent embarrassment to a relative,
"There was no bullet hole through my clothes. I shot only once."

He explained that officers were "not expected to take a part in the fighting."[74] Shirking in battle could not be hidden. Since companies represented specific communities, those who failed to perform their duty were an embarrassment to their extended kin as well as their fellow soldiers. Ras Stirman wrote a painful letter to his sister concerning their cousin Wilks:

> I suppose you have heard how he acted the day of the battle, if not I will tell you, instead of going in the ranks with us he got into a wagon and lade down. This is true. I am more deceived in him than in any boy I ever knew, he is a coward to forsake his Comrades in time of danger & worse than all his country. I wonder how Aunt Sally will receive him. If you have not heard of it before don't tell any one how you found out, but Uncle Jeff and Cousin John know how he done.[75]

Not surprisingly, those who sacrificed their lives received more than their due accord, particularly if they displayed conspicuous bravery. A soldier in the First Arkansas Mounted Rifles wrote, "Jas. Harper, Col. Churchill's Adjutant, is mortally wounded.... When young Harper fell, they went to him, but he desired them not to stop, but go on and whip them.... Brown, of the V.B.F. Guards, after he had received a mortal wound, cheered his brave boys to advance. Weaver, of Woodruff's Battery, a gallant man, fell mortally wounded from a round shot."[76] Captain William Woodruff gave his own account of the death of Lieutenant Weaver, the son of one of Little Rock's leading families: "Poor Omer Weaver fell like a hero, with his face to the foe, and died some two hours later, as befits a *man*. During the fight he refused to get under any shelter at all. No man ever died a more glorious death."[77]

Few institutions are as partisan as a local newspaper. While the Arkansas press praised the Missouri State Guard and acknowledged the deeds of the Louisianans and Texans, readers might think that Arkansans won the Battle of Wilson's Creek more or less by themselves. One correspondent asserted that the Arkansans had "saved the day," writing: "After the fight, McCulloch said, 'Pearce, you saved me and the battle; they had me down, you brought the 3d and 5th and saved me.'"[78] Although there was some controversy over the care wounded Arkansans received following the battle, newspapers downplayed or ignored the fact that the Western Army had been surprised in its camps. As was common throughout the war, newspapers wildly overestimated the enemy's numbers and losses.[79]

Within hours of the battle's end, McCulloch and Price were at odds concerning what should be done next. After occupying Springfield, Price wanted to strike north. McCulloch argued against this. He accurately predicted that such a move might enjoy initial success but was bound to come to grief because the Southerners lacked an adequate logistical base. Pearce's views are not known, but there is no evidence that he objected when McCulloch decided to end the alliance with the Missouri State Guard and withdraw with his men back across the state line into Arkansas. Within weeks, the Western Army was no more. When their enlistments expired, the Arkansas State Troops were discharged and returned to their home communities. Many re-enlisted in Confederate units, joining their fellow Arkansans in McCulloch's now veteran brigade for the Battle of Pea Ridge in March 1862—and many other fights thereafter. Writing twenty years after the war ended, Pearce provided a fitting tribute and accurate summary of the Arkansans' participation in the Wilson's Creek campaign and its relationship to later events: "The Arkansans in this battle were as brave, as chivalrous, and as successful as any of the troops engaged. They bore out, on many a hard-fought field later on in the struggle, the high hopes built upon their conduct there."[80]

Notes

"An eternal chitter chatter kept up in the galleries":
The Arkansas Secession Convention in Action,
March–June, 1861
Michael B. Dougan

1. Michael B. Dougan, *Confederate Arkansas: The People and Policies of a Frontier State in Wartime* (Tuscaloosa: University of Alabama Press, 1976), 23-34. James M. Woods, *Rebellion and Realignment: Arkansas's Road to Secession* (Fayetteville: University of Arkansas Press, 1987), 70-90.

2. Josiah Snow to Abraham Lincoln, February 25, 1864. Abraham Lincoln Papers, Library of Congress. Snow claimed Lincoln got "some ten votes."

3. Dougan, *Confederate Arkansas*, 35-46; Woods, *Rebellion*, 91-112. The John W. Brown Diary can be found at the Arkansas History Commission and in a number of university libraries.

4. Uninvestigated to date is the role of the county in Arkansas history, but for comparative purposes, consult Robert M. Ireland, *Little Kingdoms: The Counties of Kentucky, 1850-1891* (Lexington: University Press of Kentucky, 1977). Biographies on the other participants include Diane Neal and Thomas W. Kremm, *The Lion of the South: General Thomas C. Hindman* (Macon: Mercer University Press, 1993); Walter Lee Brown, *A Life of Albert Pike* (Fayetteville: University of Arkansas Press, 1997); and Elsie M. Lewis, "Robert Ward Johnson: Militant Spokesman of the Old South-West," *Arkansas Historical Quarterly* 13 (Spring 1954): 16-30.

5. Ollinger Crenshaw, "Governor Conway's Analysis and Proposed Solution of the Sectional Controversy, 1860," *Arkansas Historical Quarterly* 2 (Spring 1943): 12-19.

6. W. Buck Yearns, ed., *The Confederate Governors* (Athens: University of Georgia Press, 1985), 41-52. Also useful on Rector are Timothy P. Donovan, et al., *Governors of Arkansas: Essays in Political Biography*, 2nd edition (Fayetteville: University of Arkansas Press, 1995), 33-35, as well as entries in the online Encyclopedia of Arkansas History & Culture (www.encyclopediaofarkansas.net).

7. Dougan, *Confederate Arkansas*, 12-22; Woods, *Rebellion*.

8. Michael B. Dougan, *Community Diaries: Arkansas Newspapering, 1819–2002* (Little Rock: August House Publishers, 2003), 63-76; Michael B. Dougan, "The Little Rock Press Goes to War, 1861–1863," *Arkansas Historical Quarterly* 28 (Spring 1969): 14-27.

9. Ralph L. Goodrich Diary, November 15, 1860. Goodrich Family Papers, Arkansas History Commission, Little Rock, Arkansas.

10. Woods, *Rebellion*, 116. Woods argues that the speech was not a call for secession and labeled it the "most misconstrued speech in Arkansas history."

11. Dougan, *Confederate Arkansas*, 35-41. Woods, *Rebellion*, 113-132. The extensive Walker materials are surveyed in Ted J. Smith, "Mastering Farm and Family: David Walker as Slaveowner," *Arkansas Historical Quarterly* 58 (Spring 1999): 61-79.

12. Dougan, *Confederate Arkansas*, 41-43. Ralph Goodrich in his diary (February 5, 1861) was emphatic: "The gov. is acting the fool. He wants to precipitate the State into Revolution."

13. Dougan, *Confederate Arkansas*, 45-49. Studies include Donald E. Reynolds, *Editors Make War: Southern Newspapers in the Secession Crisis* (Nashville: Vanderbilt University Press, 1970) and Lorman A. Ratner and Dwight L. Teeter, *Fanatics and Fire-Eaters: Newspapers and the Coming of the Civil War* (Urbana: University of Illinois Press, 2003).

14. The only study on the membership of the convention is Ralph Wooster, "The Arkansas Secession Convention," *Arkansas Historical Quarterly* 13 (Autumn 1954): 172-195. While this study is still useful, more data have come to light about the finances and connections of many of the members.

15. Woods, *Rebellion*, 40.

16. Dougan, *Confederate Arkansas*, 49-51.

17. Dougan, *Confederate Arkansas*, 50-55. The persistence with which the pro-secessionist press pushed the idea of Arkansas's tie to the Deep South is in itself an indication of the relative remoteness of New Orleans and all that it represented for most Arkansans. Overwhelmingly, the newspapermen making this argument were from Kentucky or even more northerly places. Massachusetts-born Albert Pike in his extended treatment of the issues, *State or Province? Bond or Free?* (Little Rock, 1861), argued: "We cannot separate from the Cotton growing States. You might as well expect a limb severed from a human body to live. Sink or swim, persevere or perish, our destiny and theirs must be one." Woods, *Rebellion*, 151.

18. Dougan, *Confederate Arkansas*, 56.

19. Woods, *Rebellion*, 153-170. Woods highlights the contrasts and problems that Arkansas presents over these issues. Dougan, *Confederate Arkansas*, 44, 84.

20. Jason Phillips, "The Grape Vine Telegraph: Rumors and Confederate Persistence," *Journal of Southern History* 72 (November 2006): 753-788, at 787 (citing Richard T. LaPiere and Paul R. Farnsworth, *Social Psychology* (New York, 1936). Ratner and Teeter, *Fanatics*, 14, quoting the Philadelphia *Morning Pennsylvanian* on the telegraph: "Its whole stock in trade consists in the perpetual excitement of the community—in a morbid appetite for startling news and a monomania for extravagant and almost incredible rumors." Arkansas editors, not yet experienced in the wonder-working wire, learned this lesson during the first year of the war.

21. Dougan, *Confederate Arkansas*, 72.

22. Dougan, *Confederate Arkansas*, 61. This event happened two weeks before the convention reassembled, but aside from the reports of rowdiness, it did not lead to the kind of reaction that had greeted the earlier arsenal assault.

23. Quoted in Dougan, *Confederate Arkansas*, 62.

24. Quoted in Dougan, *Confederate Arkansas*, 61, from United States War Department, comp., *The War of the Rebellion: A Compilation of the Official Records of the Union and Confederate Armies* (Washington, 1880–1901), Series I, 687, and cited multiple times since accompanied by admiring prose.

25. Dougan, *Confederate Arkansas*, 62-67.

26. No time zones existed, and each town kept by means of sun dials its own town time. However, the steeple of the Christian Church contained a clock (and hence this Campbellite building was referred to as "Town Clock Church"); presumably this is the authority for the time.

27. The surviving and remarkably extensive correspondence among these delegates can be found in Dougan, *Confederate Arkansas*, 62-63.

28. Dougan, *Confederate Arkansas*, 64-67.

29. Dougan, *Confederate Arkansas*, 66-70.

30. Dougan, *Confederate Arkansas*, 66.

31. Dougan, *Confederate Arkansas*, 66-67. John W. Brown, for one, approved of the new document and planned to start up something resembling a private bank.

32. Dougan, *Confederate Arkansas*, 68-104; Thomas A. DeBlack, *With Fire and Sword: Arkansas, 1861-1874* (Fayetteville: University of Arkansas Press, 2003), 1-74.

33. Mrs. T. J. Gaughan, *Letters of a Confederate Surgeon, 1861–1865* (Camden, AR: Hurley Co., 1960), 120-121.

Domesticity Goes Public:
Southern Women and the Secession Crisis
Lisa Tendrich Frank

1. A. W. Bishop, *Loyalty on the Frontier*, 23. As quoted in Michael B. Dougan, *Confederate Arkansas: The People and Politics of a Frontier State in Wartime* (Tuscaloosa: University of Alabama Press, 1976), 62.

2. As quoted in Dougan, *Confederate Arkansas*, 62.

3. Margaret Mitchell, *Gone with the Wind* (1936; Reprint, New York: Avon Books, 1973), 8.

4. White Southern women in the pre-war years actively participated in the public sphere. See Elizabeth R. Varon, *We Mean to Be Counted: White Women and Politics in Antebellum Virginia* (Chapel Hill: University of North Carolina Press, 1998); Elizabeth R. Varon, "Tippecanoe and the Ladies, Too: White Women and Party Politics in Antebellum Virginia," *Journal of American History* 82 (September 1995): 494-521; Kirsten E. Wood, "'One Woman So Dangerous': Gender and Power in the Eaton Affair," *Journal of the Early Republic* 17 (Summer 1997): 237-275; Kirsten E. Wood, *Masterful Women: Slaveholding Widows from the American Revolution through the Civil War* (Chapel Hill: University of North Carolina Press, 2004); Daniel Kilbride, "Cultivation, Conservatism, and the

Early National Gentry: The Manigault Family and Their Circle," *Journal of the Early Republic* 19 (Summer 1999): 221-256; Cynthia A. Kierner, "Hospitality, Sociability, and Gender in the Southern Colonies," *Journal of Southern History* 62 (August 1996): 449-480; Cynthia A. Kierner, "Women's Piety Within Patriarchy: The Religious Life of Martha Hancock Wheat of Bedford County," *Virginia Magazine of History and Biography* 100 (January 1992): 79-98; Frederick A. Bode, "A Common Sphere: White Evangelicals and Gender in Antebellum Georgia," *Georgia Historical Quarterly* 79 (Winter 1995): 775-809.

5. Mary P. Ryan, *Cradle of the Middle Class: The Family in Oneida County, New York, 1790–1865* (New York: Cambridge University Press, 1981); Nancy F. Cott, *The Bonds of Womanhood: "Woman's Sphere" in New England, 1780–1835* (New Haven, CT: Yale University Press, 1977); Caroll Smith-Rosenberg, *Disorderly Conduct: Visions of Gender in Victorian America* (New York: Alfred A. Knopf, 1985); Linda K. Kerber, "Separate Spheres, Female Worlds, Women's Place: The Rhetoric of Women's History," *Journal of American History* 75 (June 1988): 9-39.

6. Barbara Welter, "The Cult of True Womanhood, 1820–1860," in *Dimity Convictions: The American Women in the Nineteenth Century* (Athens: Ohio University Press, 1976), 21-41.

7. Southern social relations were based on the status gained by race. White women had power in their households over their slaves and children. In her study of plantation women and their household relationships, Elizabeth Fox-Genovese showed that slave-holding women were not necessarily subjugated by the ideals of the Southern lady. Instead, they benefited from their roles as the heads of the domestic activities in the household. Elizabeth Fox-Genovese, *Within the Plantation Household: Black and White Women of the Old South* (Chapel Hill: University of North Carolina Press, 1988). Others also discuss white women's limited power in the Southern household. For example, see Brenda E. Stevenson, *Life in Black and White: Family and Community in the Slave South* (New York: Oxford University Press, 1996); Marli F. Weiner, *Mistresses and Slaves: Plantation Women in South Carolina, 1830–1880* (Urbana: University of Illinois Press, 1998); Stephanie McCurry, *Masters of Small Worlds: Yeoman Households, Gender Relations, and the Political Culture of the Antebellum South Carolina Low Country* (New York: Oxford University Press, 1995); Stephanie McCurry, "The Politics of Yeoman Households in South Carolina," in *Divided Houses: Gender and the Civil War*, edited by Catherine Clinton and Nina Silber (New York: Oxford University Press, 1992), 22-38; Cynthia A. Kierner, *Beyond the Household: Women's Place in the Early South, 1700–1835* (Ithaca: Cornell University Press, 1998); Laura F. Edwards, *Scarlett Doesn't Live Here Anymore: Southern Women in the Civil War Era* (Urbana: University of Illinois Press, 2000), 15-31.

8. For example, many white Southern women entered the public sphere as authors, keeping their sex secret by using pseudonyms. See Alice Fahs, *The Imagined Civil War: Popular Literature of the North and South, 1861–1865* (Chapel Hill: University of North Carolina Press, 2001), 120-149; Elizabeth Moss, *Domestic Novelists in the Old South: Defenders of Southern Culture* (Baton Rouge: Louisiana

State University Press, 1992); Anne Goodwyn Jones, *Tomorrow is Another Day: The Woman Writer in the South, 1859–1936* (Baton Rogue: Louisiana State University Press, 1981); Nina Baym, *Woman's Fiction: A Guide to Novels By and About Women in America, 1820–1870* (1978; Reprint, Chicago: University of Illinois Press, 1993); Mary Kelley, "The Literary Domestics: Private Women on a Public Stage," in *Ideas in America's Cultures: From Republic to Mass Society*, edited by Hamilton Cravens (Ames: Iowa State University Press, 1982), 83-102; Mary Kelley, *Private Woman, Public Stage: Literary Domesticity in Nineteenth Century America* (New York: Oxford University Press, 1984). Eugene Genovese discusses women's influence over their husbands in political matters. Eugene D. Genovese, "Toward a Kinder and Gentler America: The Southern Lady in the Greening of the Politics of the Old South," in *In Joy and in Sorrow: Women, Family and Marriage in the Victorian South*, edited by Carol Bleser (New York: Oxford University Press, 1991), 125-134. Similarly, LeeAnn Whites highlights "public domesticity" during the Civil War. LeeAnn Whites, *The Civil War as a Crisis in Gender: Augusta, Georgia, 1860–1890* (Athens: University of Georgia Press, 1995), 50.

    9. Although not engaged as military enemies, Northern women, like their Southern counterparts, similarly restructured their roles in society to mobilize for the Union war effort. They became nurses, fundraisers, spies, and sometimes soldiers. For discussions of Northern women during the Civil War, see Lyde Cullen Sizer, *The Political Work of Northern Women Writers and the Civil War, 1850–1872* (Chapel Hill: University of North Carolina Press, 2000); Nina Silber, *Daughters of the Union: Northern Women Fight the Civil War* (Cambridge: Harvard University Press, 2005); Jeanie Attie, *Patriotic Toil: Northern Women and the American Civil War* (Ithaca: Cornell University Press, 1998); Elizabeth D. Leonard, *All the Daring of the Soldier: Women of the Civil War Armies* (New York: W. W. Norton and Company, 1999); Elizabeth D. Leonard, *Yankee Women: Gender Battles in the Civil War* (New York: W. W. Norton & Company, 1994); Kristie Ross, "Arranging a Doll's House: Refined Women as Union Nurses," in *Divided Houses: Gender and the Civil War*, edited by Catherine Clinton and Nina Silber (New York: Oxford University Press, 1992), 97-113; Lyde Cullen Sizer, "Acting Her Part: Narratives of Union Women Spies," in *Divided Houses: Gender and the Civil War*, edited by Catherine Clinton and Nina Silber (New York: Oxford University Press, 1992), 114-133; Jeanie Attie, "Warwork and the Crisis of Domesticity in the North," in *Divided Houses: Gender and the Civil War*, edited by Catherine Clinton and Nina Silber (New York: Oxford University Press, 1992), 247-259; Mary Elizabeth Massey, *Women in the Civil War* (1966; Reprint, Lincoln: University of Nebraska Press, 1994); Judith Ann Giesberg, *Civil War Sisterhood: The U.S. Sanitary Commission and Women's Politics in Transition* (Boston: Northeastern University Press, 2000); Jane Schultz, "Inhospitable Hospital: Gender and Professionalism in Civil War Medicine," *Signs* 17 (Winter 1992): 363-392; Megan J. McClintock, "Civil War Pensions and the Reconstruction of Union Families," *Journal of American History* 83 (September 1996): 456-480; Judith Giesberg, *"Army at Home": Women and the Civil War on the Northern Home Front* (Chapel Hill: University of North Carolina Press, 2009).

10. The most prominent example of women's role in the development of Confederate nationalism is Augusta Jane Evans's novel *Macaria; or, Altars of Sacrifice*, which offered Southern women two ideals to follow in their support of the Confederacy. Evans's two main characters demonstrate how white women of privileged and poor backgrounds could make the sacrifices necessary to support the Confederacy. Augusta Jane Evans, *Macaria; or, Altars of Sacrifice* (1864; Reprint, Baton Rouge: Louisiana State University Press, 1992). On Confederate nationalism, see Gary W. Gallagher, *The Confederate War: How Popular Will, Nationalism, and Military Strategy Could Not Stave Off Defeat* (Cambridge: Harvard University Press, 1997); William Blair, *Virginia's Private War: Feeding Body and Soul in the Confederacy, 1861–1865* (New York: Oxford University Press, 1998); Anne Sarah Rubin, *A Shattered Nation: The Rise and Fall of the Confederacy, 1861–1868* (Chapel Hill: University of North Carolina Press, 2005); Drew Gilpin Faust, *Mothers of Invention: Women of the Slaveholding South in the American Civil War* (Chapel Hill: University of North Carolina Press, 1996); Drew Gilpin Faust, "Altars of Sacrifice: Confederate Women and the Narratives of War," *Journal of American History* 76 (March 1990): 1200-1228; Drew Gilpin Faust, *The Creation of Confederate Nationalism: Ideology and Identity in the Civil War South* (Baton Rouge: Louisiana State University Press, 1988); Drew Gilpin Faust, "Race, Gender, and Confederate Nationalism: William D. Washington's *Burial of Latane*," *Southern Review* 25 (Spring 1989): 297-307. Also see George C. Rable, *Civil Wars: Women and the Crisis of Southern Nationalism* (Urbana: University of Illinois Press, 1989); Victoria E. Bynum, *Unruly Women: The Politics of Social and Sexual Control in the Old South* (Chapel Hill: University of North Carolina Press, 1992); Edwards, *Scarlett Doesn't Live Here Anymore*; Catherine Clinton, *Tara Revisited: Women, War, and the Plantation Legend* (New York: Abbeville Press, 1995); LeeAnn Whites, *Gender Matters: Civil War, Reconstruction, and the Making of the New South* (New York: Palgrave Macmillan Press, 2005).

11. See Christopher J. Olsen, "Respecting 'The Wise Allotment of Our Sphere': White Women and Politics in Mississippi, 1840–1860," *Journal of Women's History* 11, 3 (Autumn 1999): 104-125; Varon, "Tippecanoe and the Ladies, Too," 494-521; Robert E. May, "Reconsidering Antebellum U.S. Women's History: Gender, Filibustering, and America's Quest for Empire," *American Quarterly* 57 (December 2005): 1155-1188.

12. Varon, "Tippecanoe and the Ladies, Too," 517.

13. Varon, "Tippecanoe and the Ladies, Too," 494-521; Olsen, "Respecting 'The Wise Allotment of Our Sphere,'" 104-125.

14. Genovese, "Toward a Kinder and Gentler America," 127.

15. Varon, "Tippecanoe and the Ladies, Too," 521.

16. Genovese, "Toward a Kinder and Gentler America," 130.

17. Varon, "Tippecanoe and the Ladies, Too," 521.

18. The most prominent diarist of the period is Mary Boykin Chesnut, *Mary Chesnut's Civil War*, edited by C. Vann Woodward (New Haven: Yale University Press, 1981). See also Emma Holmes, *The Diary of Miss Emma Holmes*, edited by John F. Marszalek (Baton Rouge: Louisiana State University Press, 1994); *Anna*

Maria Green Cook, The Journal of a Milledgeville Girl, edited by James Bonner (Athens: University of Georgia Press, 1964).

Wealthy antebellum Southern women received extensive educations. On female education in the South, see Christie Anne Farnham, *The Education of the Southern Belle: Higher Education and Student Socialization in the Antebellum South* (New York: New York University Press, 1994). Many Southern female academies offered girls a curriculum that mirrored that taken by their male counterparts. Girls attending these academies learned classic languages, higher mathematics, literature, philosophy, and other subjects. See *Augusta Chronicle & Georgia Gazette,* December 24, 1821, Volume 36, Number 21; *Augusta Chronicle and Georgia Advertiser,* October 8, 1823, Volume 38, Number 144; *Catalogue of the Instructors, Patrons and Pupils, of the LaGrange Collegiate Seminary, For Young Ladies,* 14; *Catalogue of the Instructors, Pupils and Patrons of the LaGrange Female Seminary, With a Circular Annexed for 1846, LaGrange, Georgia,* 11-12; *Catalogue of the Instructors, Patrons and Pupils of the LaGrange Female Seminary, LaGrange Georgia, for the Academical Year, 1849,* 14; *Southern Recorder,* January 2, 1830; *Augusta Chronicle-Sentinel,* January 14, 1840; *Augusta Chronicle-Sentinel,* January 21 and 25, 1840; *Third Annual Catalogue ... Washington, GA; Georgia Journal* (Milledgeville), November 7, 1831.

19. Ella Gertrude Clanton Thomas, September 17, 1864, *The Secret Eye: The Journal of Ella Gertrude Clanton Thomas, 1848–1889,* edited by Virginia Ingraham Burr (Chapel Hill: University of North Carolina Press, 1990), 236.

20. Julia Gardiner Tyler to Mother, February 3, 1861, in Katherine M. Jones, editor, *Ladies of Richmond: Confederate Capital* (New York: Bobbs-Merrill Company, Inc., 1962), 45.

21. Grace Brown Elmore, October 18, 1860, Diary and Reminiscence [type-script], South Caroliniana Library, University of South Carolina, Columbia.

22. Leora Sims to Harriet R. Palmer, December 10, 1860, in Louis P. Towles, editor, *A World Turned Upside Down: The Palmers of South Santee, 1818–1881* (Columbia: University of South Carolina Press, 1996), 278.

23. Dolly Lunt Burge, November 6, 1860, *The Diary of Dolly Lunt Burge, 1848–1879,* edited by Christine Jacobson Carter (Athens: University of Georgia Press, 1997), 111.

24. For example, see Dougan, *Confederate Arkansas,* 50.

25. Channing, *Crisis of Fear,* 178, 287; Olsen, "Respecting 'The Wise Allotment of Our Sphere.'" Genovese notes the influence and role of what he labels "extremist" women in antebellum and Civil War times. He stresses that in recognizing these Southern women, "the numbers do not matter"; the importance lies in the reality of their existence. Genovese, "Toward a Kinder and Gentler America," 133. Not all Southern women supported secession. For examples, see Thomas G. Dyer, *Secret Yankees: The Union Circle in Confederate Atlanta* (Baltimore: Johns Hopkins University Press, 1999); Jane H. Pease and William H. Pease, *A Family of Women: The Carolina Petigrus in Peace and War* (Chapel Hill: University of North Carolina Press, 1999), esp. 1-6, 140-141.

26. Grace Brown Elmore, October 18, 1860, Diary and Reminiscence [type-script], South Caroliniana Library, University of South Carolina, Columbia.

27. Ellen Sherman to Maria Ewing, May 20, 1861, Ellen Boyle Ewing Sherman Collection, Huntington Library, Ahmanson Reading Room, San Marino, California.

28. Elizabeth Paisley Dargan, ed., *The Civil War Diary of Martha Abernathy* (Beltsville, MD: Professional Printing, Inc., 1994), 1.

29. Kate Stone, May 27, 1861, *Brokenburn: The Journal of Kate Stone, 1861–1868*, edited by John Q. Anderson (Baton Rouge: Louisiana State University Press, 1972), 19.

30. Kate Thompson to Mrs. Cobb, April 15 and 17, 1861, Cobb-Erwin-Lamar Collection, Hargrett Rare Book and Manuscript Library, University of Georgia, Athens.

31. Margaret Sumner McLean, January 9, 1861, in Katherine M. Jones, editor, *Ladies of Richmond: Confederate Capital* (New York: Bobbs-Merrill Company, Inc., 1962), 34-35.

32. Emma Holmes, February 13, 1861, *Diary*, 1.

33. Cook, January 3, 1861, *Journal of a Milledgeville Girl*, 9.

34. Judith White McGuire, May 21, 1861, *Diary of a Southern Refugee During the War, by a Lady of Virginia*, edited by Jean V. Berlin (Lincoln: University of Nebraska Press, 1995), 16.

35. Thomas, July 13, 1861, *The Secret Eye*, 184.

36. Emma Mordecai to Alfred Mordecai, April 21, 1861, Mordecai Papers, Library of Congress, Washington, DC.

37. Mary Boykin Chesnut, February 18, 1861, *The Private Mary Chesnut: The Unpublished Civil War Diaries*, edited by C. Vann Woodward and Elizabeth Muhlenfeld (New York: Oxford University Press, 1984), 4.

38. Christopher J. Olsen, "Respecting 'The Wise Allotment of Our Sphere,'" 104-105.

39. *Weekly Arkansas Gazette*, June 15, 1861.

40. On the Confederate flag culture and women's role in it, see, Robert E. Bonner, *Colors and Blood: Flag Passions of the Confederate South* (Princeton, NJ: Princeton University Press, 2002), esp. 33 and 83-84.

41. Reverend Wheat to Major Wheat, May 30, 1861. As quoted in Dougan, *Confederate Arkansas*, 72.

42. Reverend Wheat to Major Wheat, May 30, 1861. As quoted in Dougan, *Confederate Arkansas*, 72.

43. Reverend Wheat to Major Wheat, May 30, 1861. As quoted in Dougan, *Confederate Arkansas*, 72. See also, Henry Morton Stanley, *Sir Henry Morton Stanley: Confederate*, edited by Nathaniel Cheairs Hughes Jr. (Baton Rouge: Louisiana State University Press, 2000), 104.

44. Henry and Drucilla Wray to Sister, April 17, 1861, Wray Papers, Georgia Historical Society, Savannah.

45. As quoted in Dougan, *Confederate Arkansas*, 69.

46. Stanley, *Sir Henry Morton Stanley*, 93-94.

47. Mrs. Allen S. Izard to Mrs. William Mason Smith, July 21, 1864, *Mason Smith Family Letters, 1860–1868*, edited by Daniel Elliott Huger Smith (Columbia: University of South Carolina Press, 1950), 116.

48. S. Emma E. Edmonds, *Nurse and Spy in the Union Army; Comprising the Adventures and Experiences of a Woman in Hospitals, Camps and Battle-fields* (Hartford: W. S. Williams & Co., 1865), 332. During the Civil War, Edmonds served as a field nurse and a spy. She also disguised herself as a man to enlist in the Union army. As Edmonds and other female Union spies reveal, Northern women also found ways to take an active part in war and other activities usually reserved for men. See Leonard, *All the Daring of the Soldier,* 170; Elizabeth R. Varon, *Southern Lady, Yankee Spy: The True Story of Elizabeth Van Lew, A Union Agent in the Heart of the Confederacy* (New York: Oxford University Press, 2003).

49. Stanley, *Sir Henry Morton Stanley,* 95.

50. See William G. Stevenson, *Thirteen Months in the Rebel Army: Being a Narrative of Personal Adventures in the Infantry, Ordnance, Cavalry, Courier, and Hospital Services; With an Exhibition of the Power, Purposes, Earnestness, Military Despotism, and Demoralization of the South* (New York: A. S. Barnes & Burr, 1862), 195.

51. Mitchell, *Gone with the Wind,* 8.

52. United Confederate Veterans Arkansas Division, *Confederate Women of Arkansas in the Civil War, 1861–1865* (Little Rock: H. G. Pugh, 1907).

Why They Fought: Arkansans Go To War, 1861
Carl H. Moneyhon

1. John A. Lynn, *The Bayonets of the Republic: Motivation and Tactics in the Army of Revolutionary France, 1791–1794* (Boulder, CO: Westview Press, 1996), 35.

2. James M. McPherson, *For Cause and Comrades: Why Men Fought in the Civil War* (New York: Oxford University Press, 1997), chapter 1.

3. McPherson, *For Cause and Comrades,* 28; James M. McCaffrey, *The Army of Manifest Destiny: The American Soldier in the Mexican War, 1846–1848* (New York: New York University Press, 1992), 31.

4. James Williamson to Dear Miss, May 2, 1862, James W. Williamson Papers, Butler Center for Arkansas Studies, Central Arkansas Library System, Little Rock.

5. Stephen T. Fair to Dear Poly, Sept. 1861, in Kate Beasley, ed., "Three Civil War Letters," *Arkansas Historical Quarterly* 3 (1944): 184.

6. Daniel E. Sutherland, ed. *Reminiscences of a Private: William E. Bevens of the First Arkansas Infantry, C.S.A.* (Fayetteville: University of Arkansas Press, 1992), 7.

7. Alex E. Spence to Sallie, May 10, 1861, in Mark K. Christ, ed., *Getting Used to Being Shot At: The Spence Family Civil War Letters* (Fayetteville: University of Arkansas Press, 2002), 4.

8. W. W. Garner to My Dear Sister, Feb. 3, 1862, "Letters of an Arkansas Confederate Soldier," *Arkansas Historical Quarterly* 2 (March 1943): 62.

9. W. L. Gammage, *The Camp, the Bivouac, and the Battle Field, Being a History of the Fourth Arkansas Regiment from Its First Organization Down to the Present Date* (Little Rock: Arkansas Southern Press, 1958, reprint of 1864 edition), 10.

10. J. G. Heaslet, "Civil War Experiences of a Benton County Youth," *Benton County Pioneer* 3 (January 1958): 4.

11. B. F. Boone to Beloved wife, Aug. 2, 1861, in Nora Boone Carlile, ed., "A Letter of Lieutenant Boone, C.S.A.," *Arkansas Historical Quarterly* 3 (1944): 64.

12. James Williamson to My Dear Father, Nov. 11, 1861, James W. Williamson Letters, Butler Center for Arkansas Studies, Central Arkansas Library System, Little Rock.

13. Wm. A. Crawford to My Dear wife & Children, April 26, 1862, in Charles G. Williams, ed., "A Saline Guard: The Civil War Letters of Col. William Ayers Crawford, C.S.A., 1861–1865, pt. II," *Arkansas Historical Quarterly* 32 (Spring 1973): 74.

14. Lewis Butler to Emma Butler, Aug. 12, 1861, in Elizabeth Paisley Huckaby and Ethel C. Simpson, eds., *Tulip Evermore: Emma Butler and William Paisley, Their Lives in Letters, 1857–1887* (Fayetteville: University of Arkansas Press, 1985), 26.

15. G. T. Whisenmate to Dear Sabra, July 28, 1861, in http://www.couchgen-web.com/civilwar/ltrwhise.htm, accessed Aug. 4, 2009.

16. Historical Census Browser http://fisher.lib.virginia.edu/collections/stats/histcensus/, accessed Aug. 11, 2009; *Biographical and Historical Memoir of Eastern Arkansas* (Chicago: Goodspeed Publishing Co., 1890), 636; *Biographical and Historical Memoir of Northeastern Arkansas* (Chicago: Goodspeed Publishing Co., 1889), 367; *Biographical History of Pulaski, Jefferson, Faulkner, Lonoke, Grant, Saline, Perry, Garland, and Hot Spring Counties, Arkansas* (Chicago: Goodspeed Publishing Co., 1889), 366-67; *Biographical and Historical Memoirs of Southern Arkansas* (Chicago: Goodspeed Publishing Co., 1890), 707.

17. *Biographical and Historical Memoir of Eastern Arkansas* (Chicago: Goodspeed Publishing Co., 1890), 636; *Biographical and Historical Memoir of Northeastern Arkansas* (Chicago: Goodspeed Publishing Co., 1889), 367; *Biographical History of Pulaski, Jefferson, Faulkner, Lonoke, Grant, Saline, Perry, Garland, and Hot Spring Counties, Arkansas* (Chicago: Goodspeed Publishing Co., 1889), 380-81; *Biographical and Historical Memoirs of Southern Arkansas* (Chicago: Goodspeed Publishing Co., 1890), 707.

18. *Biographical and Historical Memoirs of Pulaski, Jefferson, Lonoke, Faulkner, Grant, Saline, Perry, Garland and Hot Springs Counties, Arkansas* (Chicago: Goodspeed Publishing Co., 1889), 381.

19. Dorothy Stanley, ed., *The Autobiography of Sir Henry Morton Stanley* (New York: Houghton Mifflin Company, 1909), 169.

20. W. J. Peel to Lizzie, Jan. 21, 1862, in Mark Miller, *"If I should Live": A History of the Sixteenth Arkansas Confederate Infantry, 1861–1863* (Conway, AR: Arkansas Research, Inc., 2000), 10.

21. George R. Woosley to Dear Wife, Aug. 11, 1862, http://www.angelfire.com/ar2/sulphursprings/woosley.htm, accessed Aug. 4, 2009.

22. J. N. Bragg to Dear Mother, Oct. 11, 1861, in Mrs. T. J. Gaughan, *Letters of a Confederate Surgeon, 1861–65* (Camden: 1960), 17.

23. Elliott H. Fletcher to My Dear Son, Nov. 25, 1861, Elliott H. Fletcher Papers, Arkansas History Commission, Little Rock, Arkansas.

24. Nathaniel Cheairs Hughes, Jr., ed., *The Civil War Memoir of Philip Daingerfield Stephenson, D. D.* (Conway, AR: University of Central Arkansas Press, 1995), 23.

25. Dorothy Stanley, ed. *The Autobiography of Sir Henry Morton Stanley* (New York: Greenwood Press, 1969); Goodrich was traveling in the South writing about the region at the war's outbreak. He left the Guards, discharged sick, in March 1862. He later joined the U.S. Army. At the war's end, he returned to Little Rock where he served as a deputy clerk in the federal circuit and district courts and achieved some fame as a Sanskrit scholar, www.griffingweb.com/ralph_leland_goodrich.htm, accessed Aug. 26, 2009.

26. Stanley, *Autobiography*, 169.

27. S. Rowland to Dear Father, Aug. 6, 1861, http://www.couchgenweb.com/civilwar/ltr_rowland.html, accessed Aug. 4, 2009.

28. Inez E. Cline, ed., "The Memoirs of Lorenzo A. Miears of Champagnolle, Union County, Arkansas," *The Record* 17 (1966): 131.

29. Stanley, *Autobiography*, 165.

30. John Lavender, *They Never Came Back: The Story of Co. F. Fourth Arks. Infantry, C.S.A.* (Pine Bluff, AR: The Perdue Co., 1956 reprint of 1864 edition), 4.

31. Ras Stirman to Dear Sis, July 1, 1861, in Pat Carr, com., *In Fine Spirits: The Civil War Letters of Ras Stirman* (Fayetteville, AR: Washington County Historical Society, 1986), 8.

32. Peter Hotze Diary, June 19, 1861, SMC, Box 29, no. 13, Arkansas History Commission, Little Rock, Arkansas.

33. Dorothy Stanley, ed., *The Autobiography of Sir Henry Morton Stanley* (New York: Houghton Mifflin Company, 1909), 169.

34. William F. Harlow, Jr., "James Madison Hudson: Confederate Soldier," *Jefferson County Historical Quarterly* 8 (1979): 19.

35. *Weekly Arkansas Gazette* (Little Rock), June 22, 1861.

36. *Arkansas Gazette*, June 1, 1861.

37. Peter Hotze Diary, June 21, 1861, SMC Box 29, no. 13, Arkansas History Commission, Little Rock, Arkansas.

38. Stanley, *Autobiography*, 173-74.

39. Stanley, *Autobiography*, 174.

40. S. Rowland to Dear Father, Aug. 6, 1861, in http://www.couchgenweb.com/civilwar/ltr_rowland.html, accessed Aug. 4, 2009.

41. Stanley, *Autobiography*, 174; John E. Reardon to Friend, April 10, 1862, *True Democrat* (Little Rock), April 29, 1862.

42. Joseph Henry Crute, Jr., *Units of the Confederate Army* (Midlothian, VA: Derwent Books, 1987), 46-47.

43. Stanley, *Autobiography*, 168.

"A Remarkably Strong Union Sentiment":
Unionism in Arkansas in 1861
Thomas A. DeBlack

1. James M. McPherson, *Battle Cry of Freedom: The Civil War Era* (New York: Oxford University Press, 1988), 859-860.

2. McPherson, *Battle Cry*, 4-5

3. David Herbert Donald, *Lincoln* (New York: Simon & Schuster, 1995), 260.

4. William W. Freehling, *The Road to Disunion: Secessionists at Bay, 1776–1854* (New York: Oxford University Press, 1990).

5. Alan Brinkley, et al., *American History: A Survey*, 8th ed. (New York: McGraw-Hill, 1991).

6. Thomas A. DeBlack, *With Fire and Sword: Arkansas, 1861–1874* (Fayetteville: University of Arkansas Press, 2003), 5.

7. Robert W. Johnson, "Address to the People of Arkansas," January 29, 1850, reprinted in *Helena Southern Shield*, July 2, 1851.

8. *Arkansas State Gazette and Democrat*, March 1, 1850.

9. *Arkansas State Gazette and Democrat*, July 25, 1851.

10. *Helena Southern Shield*, May 11, 1850, quoting *Camden Herald*, n.d., in Walter Lee Brown, *A Life of Albert Pike* (Fayetteville: University of Arkansas Press, 1997), 263.

11. Letter dated August 13, 1854, written to an unspecified publication, probably the *New York Weekly Times*. Arkansas History Commission, Little Rock.

12. *Camden Southern Stamp*, n.d., quoted in *Helena States Rights Democrat*, July 16, 1857. Quoted in James Woods, *Rebellion and Realignment: Arkansas's Road to Secession* (Fayetteville: University of Arkansas Press, 1987), 66.

13. *Arkansas State Gazette*, February 25, 1860.

14. DeBlack, *With Fire and Sword*, 7.

15. DeBlack, *With Fire and Sword*, 2-3.

16. *Arkansas State Gazette and Democrat*, May 16, 1857.

17. DeBlack, *With Fire and Sword*, 15.

18. Jack B. Scroggs, "Arkansas in the Secession Crisis," *Arkansas Historical Quarterly* 12 (Autumn 1953): 190; James Woods, *Rebellion and Realignment: Arkansas's Road to Secession* (Fayetteville: University of Arkansas Press, 1987), 110-111.

19. Woods, *Rebellion and Realignment*, 110-111.

20. McPherson, *Battle Cry*, 232.

21. *Arkansas Gazette*, November 17, 1860.

22. Brown, *A Life of Albert Pike*, 348.

23. *Little Rock True Democrat*, November 24, 1860; *Fayetteville Arkansian*, November 24, 1860.

24. Scroggs, "Arkansas in the Secession Crisis," 190.

25. *Arkansas Gazette*, November 24, 1860. Quoted in Scroggs, "Arkansas in the Secession Crisis," 192.

26. Scroggs, "Arkansas in the Secession Crisis," 197-198; Woods, 121-122.

27. Scroggs, "Arkansas in the Secession Crisis," 195-196.

28. Woods, *Rebellion and Realignment*, 122.

29. Woods, *Rebellion and Realignment*, 123-124.

30. Scroggs, "Arkansas in the Secession Crisis," 200.

31. Scroggs, "Arkansas in the Secession Crisis," 200; Woods, *Rebellion and Realignment*, 128.

32. Calvin Collier, *First In–Last Out: The Capitol Guards, Ark. Brigade* (Little Rock: Pioneer Press, 1961), 4.

33. DeBlack, *With Fire and Sword*, 22.

34. *The War of the Rebellion: A Compilation of the Official Records of the Union and Confederate Armies*, 4 series, 70 vols. (Washington, DC: Government Printing Office, 1880–1901) series I, I: 640, 644-645.

35. Collier, *First In–Last Out*, 6-7; DeBlack, *With Fire and Sword*, 22.

36. Quoted in DeBlack, *With Fire and Sword*, 22-23.

37. *Official Records* I, I: 644-645.

38. DeBlack, *With Fire and Sword*, 22, 24.

39. Woods, *Rebellion and Realignment*, 130-131.

40. David Herbert Donald, *Lincoln* (London: Jonathan Cape, 1995), 283.

41. The best account of the first secession convention is in Woods, *Rebellion and Realignment*, 137-146.

42. *Journal of Both Sessions of the Convention of the State of Arkansas* (Little Rock, 1861), 61. Quoted in Scroggs, "Arkansas in the Secession Crisis," 214.

43. Woods, *Rebellion and Realignment*, 146.

44. *Journal of Both Sessions*, 55.

45. DeBlack, *With Fire and Sword*, 25.

46. Woods, *Rebellion and Realignment*, 147.

47. *Official Records* I, I: 687.

48. John Brown Diary, April 20, 1861, Kie Oldham Collection, Arkansas History Commission, Little Rock.

49. *Arkansas Gazette*, April 20, 1861.

50. Woods, *Rebellion and Realignment*, 157-158.

51. *Journal of the Convention*, 123. Quoted in Scroggs, "Arkansas in the Secession Crisis," 223.

52. Woods, *Rebellion and Realignment*, 158-160; DeBlack, *With Fire and Sword*, 27-28.

53. Danley to William W. Mansfield, April 23, 1861. Mansfield Papers, Arkansas History Commission, Little Rock. Quoted in Woods, *Rebellion and Realignment*, 161.

54. Woods, *Rebellion and Realignment*, 162.

55. Ted R. Worley, "The Arkansas Peace Society of 1861: A Study in Mountain Unionism," in *The Journal of Southern History* 24 (November 1958): 445-446.

56. Worley, "The Arkansas Peace Society of 1861," 446-449.

57. Worley, "The Arkansas Peace Society of 1861," 449-451.

58. Worley, "The Arkansas Peace Society of 1861," 450-451.

59. Worley, "The Arkansas Peace Society of 1861," 451-453.

60. Worley, "The Arkansas Peace Society of 1861," 453-454

61. Worley, "The Arkansas Peace Society of 1861," 454-456.

62. DeBlack, *With Fire and Sword*, 31.

63. Carl H. Moneyhon, "Disloyalty and Class Consciousness in Southwestern Arkansas, 1862–1865," in *Arkansas Historical Quarterly* 52 (Autumn 1993): 223-243.

64. Moneyhon, "Disloyalty and Class Consciousness," 225, 228.

65. Brown Diary, March 19, 1863.

66. Moneyhon, "Disloyalty and Class Consciousness," 235.

67. Moneyhon, "Disloyalty and Class Consciousness," 229-230.

68. Frank Arey, "The Skirmish at McGrew's Mill," *Clark County Historical Journal* (2000): 63-66.

69. Moneyhon, "Disloyalty and Class Consciousness," 230-238.

70. Moneyhon, "Disloyalty and Class Consciousness," 37-38, 40; Brown Diary, March 19, 1863.

71. *Washington Telegraph*, January 28, 1863; Brown Diary, February 26, 1863; Sam Scott to Harris Flanagin, April 1863, Kie Oldham Collection, Arkansas History Commission, Little Rock. All quoted in Moneyhon, "Disloyalty and Class Consciousness."

72. Moneyhon, "Disloyalty and Class Consciousness," 242.

73. Quoted in DeBlack, *With Fire and Sword*, 99.

74. Maurice Smith to Harris Flanagin, n.d., in the Smith Family Papers Collection, Butler Center for Arkansas Studies, Little Rock.

75. Smith to Flanagin.

"When the Arks. boys goes by they take the rags off the bush": Arkansans in the Wilson's Creek Campaign of 1861
William Garrett Piston

1. John Johnson to Dear Mother, July 23, 1861, John Johnson Civil War Letters, Arkansas History Commission, Little Rock.

2. John Johnson to Dear Wife and Children, July 28, 1861, John Johnson Civil War Letters.

3. "Family Record"; John Johnson to Dear Wife and Children, July 22, 1861, John Johnson Civil War Letters.

4. Technically, they served in the Provisional Army of the Confederate States, as distinct from the Confederacy's small regular army.

5. W. E. Woodruff, *With the Light Guns; Reminiscences of Eleven Arkansas, Missouri and Texas Light Batteries, in the Civil War* (Little Rock: Central Publishing Company, 1903), 7-8; "Volunteers," *Arkansas True Democrat*, April 25, 1861.

6. Michael B. Dougan, *Confederate Arkansas: The People and Policies of a Frontier State in Wartime* (Tuscaloosa: University of Alabama Press, 1976), 39-63.

7. Dougan, *Confederate Arkansas*, 65-67; Woodruff, *With the Light Guns*, 17-20.

8. "From Johnson County," *Arkansas True Democrat*, April 25, 1861; "Mass Meeting in Calhoun County," *Arkansas True Democrat*, May 2, 1861. Additional examples from the April 25 issue include "Mass Meeting in Dyer Township, Saline County," "To the People of Arkansas," "Public Meeting in Pope County," "Mass Meeting in Pulaski County," and "From Saline County." In the May 2 issue, see also "Public Meeting in Lawrence County," "Public Meeting in Arkansas County," "Meeting at Waldron," "Mass Meeting," and "Mass Meeting in White County."

9. Flanagin was elected governor of Arkansas in 1862. Amy Jean Greene, "Governor Harris Flanagin," typescript, Harris Flanagin Papers, Arkansas History Commission, Little Rock.

10. Angie Lewis McRae, "Genl. D. McRae, White County Man," Dandridge McRae Biography, Small Manuscript Collection, Arkansas History Commission; Faye O. Strother, "An Arkansas General," *Arkansas Democrat Magazine* 12 (Dec. 1962).

11. Churchill was governor of Arkansas from 1881 to 1883. William S. Speer, ed., *The Encyclopedia of the New West* (Marshall, TX: U.S. Biographical Publishing Company, 1881), 18-19.

12. Wesley Thurman Leeper, *Rebels Valiant: Second Arkansas Mounted Rifles (Dismounted)* (Little Rock: Pioneer Press, 1964), 15.

13. John F. Walter, "Capsule Histories of Arkansas Military Units," typescript, John K. Hulston Library, Wilson's Creek National Battlefield, Republic, Missouri.

14. *Arkansas True Democrat*, July 4, 1861.

15. For a full discussion of "corporate honor," see William Garrett Piston, "The 1st Iowa Volunteers: Honor and Community in a Ninety-Day Regiment," *Civil War History* 44 (March 1998): 5-23.

16. Leeper, *Rebels Valiant*, 25.

17. "Carroll County, Ark.," *Arkansas True Democrat*, July 4, 1861.

18. "Flag Presentation," *Arkansas True Democrat*, June 6, 1861. Robert Neill, a soldier in the ranks, wrote about the ceremony to his father on May 30, 1861: "The troops were paraded on St. John's College grounds (our encampment) this evening and presented with a flag, by Miss Faulkner, daughter of Sandy of 'Arkansas Traveller' notoriety. Captain Churchill received the banner and replied through Lieut. Co. Matlock. The scene was imposing though I must say the reply to the ladies fell far short of the presentation address." Charles H. Warner and A. A. McGinnis, comps., "Captain Gibb's Company, C.S.A.," *The Independence County Chronicle* 2: 50.

19. N. B. Pearce, "Price's Campaign of 1861," *Publications of the Arkansas Historical Society* 4 (1917), 332-34; William Royston Geies, "The Confederate Military Forces in the Trans-Mississippi West, 1861–1865; A Study in Command," PhD diss., University of Texas at Austin, 1974, 8.

20. The Totten Battery adopted its title to honor Dr. William Totten, a Little Rock resident, and his son, Captain James Totten, who commanded the federal arsenal at Little Rock. Captain Totten's withdrawal had averted civil war, and most Arkansans expected him to side with the South. When Totten remained in the U.S. Army, the artillerists rechristened themselves the Pulaski Light Battery, after their county. Woodruff, *With the Light Guns*, 9. For a complete order of battle, see William Garrett Piston and Richard W. Hatcher III, *Wilson's Creek: The Second Battle of the Civil War and the Men Who Fought It* (Chapel Hill: University of North Carolina Press, 2000), 335-38.

21. Pat Carr, *In Fine Spirits: The Civil War Letters of Ras Stirman with Historical Comments by Pat Carr* (Fayetteville: Washington County Historical Society, n.d.), 8. Punctuation corrected.

22. John Johnson to Dear Wife and Children, June 14, 1861, John Johnson Civil War Letters, Arkansas History Commission, Little Rock.

23. "A Correspondent," *Arkansas True Democrat*, May 6, 1861; "A Volunteer," *Arkansas True Democrat*, June 30, 1861.

24. Dandridge McRae to Wife, May 4, 1861, Dandridge McRae Papers, Arkansas History Commission, Little Rock.

25. Muster Rolls—Companies A, B, C, McRae's Battalion, Ark. Volunteers; Muster Roll—Captain Park's Company D, First Regiment Arkansas Volunteers; Muster Roll, Buchanan's Co. K, 1st Reg. Inf. Ark. Vol.; Descriptive List of Cap. Lawrence's Company in Regiment Arks. Infantry; Report of Arms, equipment, etc., Company I, Camp Walker; Muster Roll—Hill's Co., Ark. Mounted Inf. Vol., all in Dandridge McRae Papers, Arkansas History Commission, Little Rock.

26. Report of Arms, equipment, etc., Company I, Camp Walker, in Dandridge McRae Papers, Arkansas History Commission, Little Rock.

27. Woodruff, *With the Light Guns*, 20; Carr, *In Fine Spirits*, 12.

28. Pearce, "Price's Campaign of 1861," 342.

29. Descriptive List of Cap. Lawrence's Company in Regiment Arks. Infantry, in Dandridge McRae Papers, Arkansas History Commission, Little Rock.

30. For a full discussion of these events, see Piston and Hatcher, *Wilson's Creek*, Chapters 2-5.

31. Carr, *In Fine Spirits*, 11.

32. John Johnson to Dear Wife and Children, July 28, 1861, John Johnson Civil War Letters, Arkansas History Commission, Little Rock.

33. U.S. War Department, *The War of the Rebellion: A Compilation of the Official Records of the Union and Confederate Armies* (Washington, DC: Government Printing Office, 1880–1901), Series 1, Vol. 3:38-39, 607; hereafter cited as *Official Records*.

34. John J. Walker to W. W. Mansfield, July 31, 1861, W. W. Mansfield Letters, Arkansas History Commission, Little Rock.

35. Piston and Hatcher, *Wilson's Creek*, 134-37; Pearce, "Price's Campaign of 1861," 338-39.

36. Piston and Hatcher, *Wilson's Creek*, 138-58.

37. Dandridge McRae to Wife, Aug. 6, 1861, Dandridge McRae Papers, Arkansas History Commission, Little Rock.

38. Woodruff, *With the Light Guns*, 37.

39. Dandridge McRae to Wife, August 6, 1861, Dandridge McRae Papers, Arkansas History Commission, Little Rock.

40. Harris Flanagin to Dear Wife, August 6, 1861, Harris Flanagin Papers, Arkansas History Commission, Little Rock.

41. Carr, *In Fine Spirits*, 16.

42. Dandridge McRae to Wife, August 6, 1861, Dandridge McRae Papers, Arkansas History Commission, Little Rock. The content of this letter suggests that McRae wrote it on August 9 but misdated it August 6.

43. Pearce, "Price's Campaign of 1861," 341.

44. In addition to Piston and Hatcher, *Wilson's Creek*, readers should consult Edwin C. Bearss, *The Battle of Wilson's Creek* (Bozeman, MT: Artcraft Printing, 1975), the pioneering study of the engagement.

45. N. B. Pearce, "Arkansas Troops in the Battle of Wilson's Creek," *Battles and Leaders of the Civil War* (New York: Century, 1887–1888), 1: 298; Pearce, "Price's Campaign of 1861," 341.

46. *Official Records*, 3:121.

47. *Official Records*, 3:120-25; "Narrative of the Battle of Oak Hills," Dandridge McRae Papers, Arkansas History Commission, Little Rock.

48. William E. Woodruff Jr. to Dear Father, August 11, 1861, *Arkansas True Democrat*, August 22, 1861.

49. *Official Records*, 3:111-12.

50. Piston and Hatcher, *Wilson's Creek*, 221-31.

51. Pearce's battle report, *Official Records*, 3:122, states: "Early in the action Captain Jefferson was sent to reconnoiter the enemy and was taken prisoner." The direction of Jefferson's investigation is unclear, and this lone action hardly constituted adequate gathering of intelligence.

52. Piston and Hatcher, *Wilson's Creek*, 246-61.

53. *Official Records*, 3:109-12.

54. *Official Records*, 3:112-13; Piston and Hatcher, *Wilson's Creek*, 273.

55. *Official Records*, 3:121. The second position of Woodruff's artillery is uncertain. It may have been upon ground that was graded level when a railroad was built through the battlefield in 1870.

56. See "Latest from Missouri," *Arkansas True Democrat*, Aug. 22, 1861, for several separate witnesses to Pearce's bravery. See also the battle reports of Gratiot and Dockery, *Official Records*, 3:123-25.

57. Pearce, "Arkansas Troops in the Battle of Wilson's Creek," 302-3.

58. Carr, *In Fine Spirits*, 18-19.

59. *Official Records*, 3:123.

60. Pearce, "The Arkansas Troops at Wilson's Creek," 303.

61. Harris Flanagin, letter fragment, Harris Flanagin Papers, Arkansas History Commission, Little Rock.

62. *Official Records*, 3:122.

63. "Extracts from a Letter Written at Springfield, Mo., by Dr. W.A. Cantrell," *Arkansas True Democrat*, Aug. 29, 1861. Interestingly, John Johnson,

one of the fatalities in the battle, had written earlier: "We have got no surgeon in our regiment worth one cent. I think Dr. Cantrell is the poorest chance I ever saw." John Johnson to Dear Wife and Children, July 22, 1861, John Johnson Civil War Letters, Arkansas History Commission, Little Rock.

64. Warner and McGinnis, "Captain Gibb's Company, C.S.A.," 46–48.

65. *Official Records*, 3:110.

66. *Official Records*, 3:111.

67. *Official Records*, 3:124-25.

68. *Official Records*, 3:126.

69. *Official Records*, 3:122; Frank Rector to Mrs. C. B. Johnson, n.d., in "Latest from Missouri," *Arkansas True Democrat*, Aug. 22, 1861. Pearce's report appeared in the *True Democrat* on August 29, 1861.

70. For a full discussion of press reportage see Brian Dirk, "'We have Whipped Them Beautifully': The Arkansas Press and Wilson's Creek," *Missouri Historical Review* 84 (April 1990): 270–92.

71. See for example the very detailed "Official Report of killed, wounded and missing, at the Battle of Oak Hills, Aug. 10, Near Springfield, Mo.," *Arkansas True Democrat*, Aug. 29, 1861.

72. John R. Gratiot to editor, Washington, Arkansas, *Telegraph*, clipping in Third Arkansas Infantry file, John K. Hulston Library, Wilson's Creek National Battlefield, Republic, Mo.

73. J. M. Bailey, "1861," *Confederate Veteran Papers*, Rare Book, Manuscript, and Special Collections, Duke University, Durham, NC.

74. Harris Flanagin to M. E. Flanagin, Sept. 15, 1861, Harris Flanagin Papers, Arkansas History Commission, Little Rock.

75. Carr, *In Fine Spirits*, 21.

76. Letter from "C.A.C." in "Latest from Missouri," *Arkansas True Democrat*, Aug. 22, 1861. The V.B.F. Guards were the Van Buren Frontier Guards.

77. William E. Woodruff Jr. to Dear Father, Aug. 11, 1861, *Arkansas True Democrat*.

78. "Latest from Missouri," *Arkansas True Democrat*, Aug. 22, 1861.

79. Dirk, "The Arkansas Press and Wilson's Creek," 289–92.

80. Pearce, "Arkansas Troops in the Battle of Wilson's Creek," 303.

Index